God
Delivers
Me

God Delivers Me

A Model From Strengthening the Black Church For the 21st Century

Jacqulyn Brown Thorpe, Editor

Abingdon Press
Nashville

God Delivers Me

CONTENTS

ILLUSTRATIONS AND TABLES

LIST OF ACRONYMS

Black Methodist for Church Renewal—BMCR

Congregational Resource Center—CRC

Ethnic Local Church—ELC

Ethnic Minority Local Church—EMLC

Partner Congregation—PC

Strengthening the Black Church for the 21st Century—SBC21

United Methodist Church—UMC

General Board of Discipleship—GBOD

PREFACE

When a people have a vision, it must be shared.
When a people have a story, it must be told.

This particular story told at this particular time is filled with passion, holy boldness, gifts of the Spirit, affirmations, and a rejoicing that fills us up. We hope that *God Delivers Me: A Model from Strengthening the Black Church for the 21st Century* also fills you up.

There are so many ways that we can share God's word and God's love. This book is full of how one group of people who believe that there is a different way to make disciples for Jesus Christ in their time and space are living out their calls.

It was in early 2006 when Fred Allen of The United Methodist Publishing House invited me to be the senior editor of this fully funded writing project that the editorial team of the national Strengthening The Black Church for the 21st Century committee wanted published. I was both intrigued and challenged by this invitation. We started immediately to plan how and who could make this a reality. I had heard of the SBC21 committee in my own Baltimore-Washington Conference, but I knew very little about the SBC21 ministries across the country.

The year 2007 was filled with administrative duties, committee meetings, conferences, research, and information gathering that led to the selection of the writers for this book. The Contributors section introduces these writers, who are skilled and gifted United Methodist church leaders. Our story is told through their voices. It is my hope that you know at least one of us and that you will want to talk to us about how you can reshape your ministry into a distinctive and culturally relevant experience that follows the model we introduce in this book.

The purpose of this book is to introduce the ministry and mission of the SBC21 that reaches across many jurisdictions, to teach laity to find religious guidance and strength for daily living, and to present a model of ministry in which Christ is our center for hope, healing, and wholeness.

The powerful DVD is a companion to this book that explains, cele-brates, and offers an updated version of the SBC21 project. We are grate-ful to Pamela Crosby and Cheryl A. Stevenson for their work on the DVD. The comprehensive appendix further strengthens the power of this book.

We have put ourselves out on the front lines of mission and ministry, and this is only the beginning of what we hope will influence you to use the SBC21 model to build vital congregations. I believe that we are liv-ing in an era when our church must open itself to change. These are trou-bling times for many of our churches because we are struggling to figure out what we need to do to keep our United Methodist Churches strong and vital. This book addresses these issues, and it makes me feel hopeful for the future.

SBC21 has been a builder of self-esteem, healthy relating among Christians, and has helped a people who have frequently asked the ques-tion, "Where do I stand?" SBC21 teaches churches to maintain integrity and to stand strong. I am blessed to be the editor of this critical assess-ment that gives a holistic view of the Action Plans approved by the 1996, 2000, and 2004 General Conferences of The United Methodist Church.

Jonathan D. Keaton, resident Bishop of the Michigan Episcopal Area and chair of the SBC21 Coordinating Committee, provides the Intro-duction to this work. Chapter 1, by Youtha Hardman-Cromwell, gives a four-century review of Blacks in Methodism prior to the initiation of the SBC21 project in 1996. Chapter 2, by Dorothy Watson Tatem and Cheryl A. Stevenson, chronicles the spiritual and community formation of several congregations using anecdotal reflections. Dorothy Watson Tatem describes in detail what we mean by the description "vital con-gregation" in chapter 3. Chapter 4, by Cynthia Hopson, tells why the Congregational Resource Centers and the Partner Churches are critical to the initiative and what differences they make. In chapter 5, F. Douglas Powe, Jr. outlines how leadership, planning, worship, faith formation, and outreach when viewed evangelistically can create a vital church. Fred Smith, Jr. begins chapter 6 by reframing the discussion as we move forward from vital congregations to unity of the beloved community as a gift to the Church. Then he assesses the SBC21 training events pro-viding insights and learnings. In the final chapter bishops Jonathan D. Keaton, Peter D. Weaver, and James R. King further warm our soul by their positive affirmations for the future.

There really is no better way to strengthen our churches than to "go and make disciples of all nations, baptizing them in the name of the Father, Son, and Holy Spirit, teaching them to obey the commands of Jesus Christ," assured that God delivers us.

Sincerely,
Jacqulyn Brown Thorpe, Senior Editor
Lecturer, Religious Education
Howard University School of Divinity, Washington, D.C.

ACKNOWLEDGMENTS

This text is the realization of the visionary leadership of Bishop Jonathan D. Keaton, Michigan Area, and chair of the Coordinating Committee of Strengthening the Black Church for the 21st Century. He believed that the program needed to be placed in text form in order that all local congregations of The United Methodist Church and beyond would have ready access to strategies that would enable them to become vital congregations now and well into this century. The bishop has contributed to the writing in *God Delivers Me* and is a member of the editorial team.

Much gratitude is extended to the original members of the study panel: Bishop Woodie W. White, chairperson; Douglas Fitch; Gilbert Caldwell; Karen Collier; Tyrone Gordon; Carolyn Johnson; Delores Queen; Ernest Swiggett; Bishop Peter Weaver; Trudie Kibble Reed. We are also grateful for the team responsible for crafting the original innovative plan for SBC21: David White, team leader; Walter Kimbrough; Ruth M. Lawson; Delano McIntosh; Nelda Barrett Murraine.

We are deeply grateful to Bishop Peter D. Weaver, Boston Area, and Bishop James R. King, Louisville Area, for their ongoing support, work on behalf of SBC21 and for their written contributions in this book.

Gratitude is generously expressed to the Evaluation Team of Strengthening the Black Church for the 21st Century. Dorothy Watson Tatem, chair; Bishop Jonathan D. Keaton; Rubielee L. Addison; Carnell Scott; Fred A. Allen; James C. Fields Jr.; Erin Hawkins; Frances Jett; Diane Johnson; and Andrea Middleton King were the persons who crafted the initial outlines for this book and set its direction.

We thank the SBC21 Coordinating Committee (2004–2008; see appendix) for their input in broadening concepts, deepening dialogue, and giving continual support in the writing of this book.

Cheryl A. Stevenson, SBC21 National Coordinator, contributed to the writing and along with administrative assistant, Pamela Holman, facilitated research and other critical resources for this text.

The voices of innumerable women and men can be heard in these pages. These are the persons in the local churches; we thank them for their labors in the transformation of their local congregations. They have participated in SBC21 as Congregational Resource Centers and as Partner Churches. Much thanks is given to them for their efforts in local church revitalization in order that the Kingdom of God might be manifested here on earth. A very special word of gratitude must be expressed to the senior editor the Reverend Jacqulyn Thorpe of Howard University Divinity School. Her expertise, experience, patience, and comprehension of SBC21 were invaluable in moving this book from outline to manuscript. We are indebted to the academics that gave of their time and skill as researchers and writers to the text. These persons are: Karen F. Williams, copy editor; Dr. Youtha Hardman-Cromwell, Wesley Theological Seminary; Dr. Cynthia Bond Hopson, Assistant General Secretary of the Black College Fund and Ethnic Concerns, General Board of Higher Education and Ministry; Dr. Fred Douglas Smith, Jr., Wesley Theological Seminary; and Dr. Douglas F. Powe, Jr., Saint Paul School of Theology. The enthusiasm and commitment of these persons to excellence remains inspiring.

We thank Pamela Crosby for her vibrant creativity in producing the DVD that accompanies this book.

Appreciation is expressed to the following resource persons and their general agencies. Each representative has given precious input and support throughout this enterprise: Clauzell Williams, General Council on Finance and Administration; Frances Jett Roberts, General Board of Church and Society; Lillian Smith, General Board of Discipleship-Division on Ministries with Young People; Cheryl Walker, General Board of Discipleship-Office of African American Ministries; Clarence Brown, General Board of Higher Education and Ministry; Ronald Coleman, General Board of Pensions and Health Benefits; James C. Fields, Jr., General Commission on Christian Unity and Interreligious Concerns; Newtonia Coleman, United Methodist Communications; Erin Hawkins, General Commission on Religion and Race; Mary White, General Commission on the Status and Role of Women; Diane Johnson, General Board of Global Ministries; and Andrea Middleton King, General Commission on United Methodist Men.

Finally, we can never adequately express our gratitude to Dr. Fred A. Allen, Executive Director-African American Initiatives and International

Outreach of The United Methodist Publishing House. He grasped the vision for *God Delivers Me*, located the senior editor, writers, and guided the editorial team through the process of publication. Dr. Allen models the quintessential dynamic of the partnership that can exist between a general church agency (in this case, The United Methodist Publishing House) and a program of the general church. He is a key member of the Evaluation and Editorial teams of SBC21.

Above all, we thank God for the blessings of this work.

Dr. Dorothy Watson Tatem
Eastern Pennsylvania Conference
Chair, SBC21 Editorial Team

CONTRIBUTORS

FRED ALLEN, D.Min., is an elder and member of the New York Annual Conference who received his degree from Drew University School of Theology in Madison, New Jersey. He has over thirty years experience as a professional minister, manager, administrator, and communicator in Christian institutions including local church pastorates, denominational national program agencies and para-church organizations. Currently, he is executive director of the African American Initiative and International Outreach at The United Methodist Publishing House. A native of Nashville, Tennessee, he is married to Christine and the father of four children.

YOUTHA HARDMAN-CROMWELL, Ph.D., is an elder in the Virginia Conference. She serves on the Board of Ministry and is Conference Chair of the Order of Elders. She is the director of the Practice in Ministry and Mission Program at Wesley Theological Seminary and associate professor of Practice in Ministry and Mission. Previously she served on the staff of Howard University School of Divinity and as pastor of Woodlawn United Methodist Church, Alexandria, Virginia.

She adds to her published work of various articles and book chapters, retreats and workshop presentations for churches and other organizations. Also, she organized Youtha & Friends, a drama group that performs "God's Trombones with Negro Spirituals."

She and her husband Oliver Cromwell, a retired government public affairs officer, have one grandchild, Tiffany, and four adult children: Darnell, Dwayne, Debra Whitten, and Michael Cromwell. Debra is also an elder in the United Methodist Church, Greater New Jersey Conference.

CYNTHIA A. BOND HOPSON, Ph.D., is assistant general secretary for the Black College Fund and Ethnic Concerns at the United Methodist Church's General Board of Higher Education and Ministry in Nashville, Tennessee. She was associate professor of journalism at The University of Memphis before coming to her present position. She has been named to Who's Who Among America's Teachers and is the author of *Wiggle Tales*, *Times of Challenge and Controversy* and *Bad Hair Days, Rainy Days and Mondays: Wisdom and Encouragement to Lift a Woman's Spirit.* She and her husband, Roger, a United Methodist minister, live in Lebanon, Tennessee and they have two children and three grandchildren.

JONATHAN D. KEATON, S.T.D., was named resident bishop of the Michigan Area of The United Methodist Church effective September 1, 2004. He currently chairs the Strengthening the Black Church for the 21st Century. He was elected to the episcopacy in 1996 and served eight years as resident bishop of the Ohio East Area.

Prior to his election to the episcopacy in 1996, he served on the conference staff responsible for monitoring the church's stand on social issues providing support and encouragement for ethnic local churches and promoting spiritual formation.

He attended Garrett-Evangelical Theological Seminary, where he earned a Master of Divinity, and Doctorate of Sacred Theology. He and his wife Beverly have three children and one grandchild.

JAMES R. KING is a resident bishop of Kentucky who has coauthored *365 Meditations for Men.* He graduated from the Interdenominational Theological Center in Atlanta. He and his wife Margaret "Rose" Hayden have three adult children.

F. DOUGLAS POWE, JR., Ph.D., is the Assistant Professor of Evangelism, E. Stanley Jones Chair at Saint Paul School of Theology in Kansas City, Missouri. He attended Ohio Wesleyan University, Delaware, Ohio where he graduated with his B.A. in 1987. In 1998, he graduated from Candler School of Theology with his Master of Divinity. In 2004, he received his Ph.D. in Theological Studies at Emory University. He is coauthor with H. Henry Knight III of *Transforming Evangelism: The Wesleyan Way of Sharing* (Discipleship Resources, 2006). He is married to Rev. Sherri E. Wood-Powe, the Pastor of Saint Paul A.M.E. Church in Olathe, Kansas. They have one son, Frederick Douglas Powe III.

DOROTHY WATSON TATEM, D. Min., presently serves as the Director of the Office of Urban and Global Ministries of the Eastern Pennsylvania Conference of The United Methodist Church. She is a member of various boards and agencies including Strengthening the Black Church for the 21st Century and the General Commission on Religion and Race; she is also a trustee at Albright College in Reading, Pennsylvania. Dr. Tatem has formerly pastured both suburban and urban churches that experienced growth in community partnerships, ministries, real estate acquisitions and membership/worship attendance. She perceives preaching as a dynamic vehicle to proclaim the reality of God.

JACQULYN BROWN THORPE, M.R.E., is a Deacon In Full Connection, a Christian education consultant, and an adjunct faculty member of Religious Education at Howard University School of Divinity in Washington, D.C., which is her primary appointment. Her corollary appointment is at North Bethesda United Methodist Church in Bethesda, Maryland. Graduated from Wesley Theological Seminary, she has extensive experience serving in local United Methodist Churches in the Baltimore-Washington Conference, and she served for eight years on the Curriculum Resources Committee of The General Board of Discipleship.

She is widely published in The United Methodist Church and other denominations, writing curriculum resources for all ages as well as scholarly articles in The Journal of Religious Thought at Howard. She is coauthor of *The Web of Women's Leadership: Recasting Congregational Ministry* (Abingdon, 2001).

A native of Louisville, Kentucky, she and her husband Marvin, a retired army officer, live in Bethesda, Maryland and they have four adult children.

FRED SMTH, JR., Ph.D., an Elder in the Baltimore-Washington Conference is associate professor of Urban Ministry and associate director of the Practice of Ministry and Mission at Wesley Theological Seminary in Washington DC. He was educated at Harvard College and earned his B.A., at Perkins School of Theology of Southern Methodist University with his Master of Divinity (cum laude), and received his Ph.D. at Emory in 1997. He had directed a number of national initiatives and he is widely published and has authored and coauthored many books, articles, reports, and curriculums. He is coauthor of *Black Religious Experience: Conversation on Double-Consciousness and the Works of Grant Shockley.*

CHERYL A. STEVENSON, a native of Wichita, Kansas is the national coordinator for Strengthening the Black Church for the 21st Century. In 2001 she left a fourteen-year career as a personnel and customer service representative with the Internal Revenue Service to give her knowledge, skills, and abilities in areas that would contribute to the ministries of The United Methodist Church. She is married to Louis and they have one beautiful daughter.

PETER D. WEAVER, who served as president of the Council of Bishops from 2004–2006 is quoted as saying, "I've yearned simply to be a disciple of Jesus which I believe is simply the highest honor that can be given to anyone." He is currently located in the Lawrence, Massachusetts Area. He holds many honors, is widely published, and well traveled. He received his Doctor of Theology from Boston University. He and his wife, Linda, have eight daughters and four grandchildren. He enjoys time with his family, water sports, playing the trombone, and woodworking.

INTRODUCTION

Jonathan D. Keaton

No statement from the life and lips of folk in the Black Church is more real than the witness or testimony "God delivers me." Though racism and its antecedents still flourish, new ideas and movements emerge in every age "to make the wounded whole." One story from General Conference 2000 in Cleveland, Ohio demonstrates the value and validity of liberating moments.

General Conference 2000 planned a service of repentance and reconciliation. We wanted to repent and reconcile with Black folk who left, namely the African Methodist Episcopal Church, the African Methodist Episcopal Zion Church, and the Christian Methodist Episcopal Church. Black folk who stayed rejoiced. At the turn of the century our denomination stepped forward to right historic wrongs. Trouble arose when "those who stayed" desired the same recognition in this denominational apologia. Their efforts were largely rebuffed. As a result, lines were drawn. If a just compromise could not be found, the service seemed headed for disruption via the absence of Black folk, presence without participation, signage of some kind, and so forth. To a small degree, most of these responses occurred. Before the service began, planners of the service offered "those who stayed" an olive branch by allowing the Rev. McAllister Hollins, Senior Pastor of Ben Hill United Methodist Church in Atlanta, Georgia to offer a statement of protest on behalf of Black folk who stayed. Some Black folk wept. Others refused to attend. Still others participated with a heavy heart. Nevertheless, they were buoyed by a word spoken to the whole Church on behalf of those who stayed. One might conclude that the whole offered its African American constituency another olive branch in General Conference 2000. It adopted legislation to strengthen the Black Church for the twenty-first century for another Quadrennium.

Strengthening the Black Church for the 21st Century (SBC21) represents the latest stance taken by The United Methodist Church (UMC) and its predecessor bodies on behalf of Black folk. It will not be the last.

Depending on the mind of the General Conference, movements in our country and world, successful advocacy for initiatives, programs, and emphases required to nurture the Black Church rise and fall like "hope deferred." Following are stories of deliverance and liberation; one necessitates the other.

When the famous 1784 Christmas Conference convened in Baltimore to create the Methodist Church in America, significant decisions were made. Inspired by John Wesley's description of slavery as "that execrable villainy which is the scandal of religion" and American slavery, "as the vilest that ever saw the sun," our founding fathers and mothers opposed slavery wholeheartedly. In part, they stated,

> We view it as contrary to the Golden Law of God on which hang all the Laws and the Prophets and the inalienable rights of mankind, as well as every principle of the revolution to hold in the deepest abasement in a more abject slavery than is perhaps to be found in any part of the world except America . . . we therefore think it is our bounded duty to take immediately some effectual method to extirpate this abomination among us.[1]

As a result, Blacks joined the Methodist Church in droves. Here was a church that preached Jesus and him crucified. The church stood up for the liberation of members kissed by the sun and consigned to a so-called life sentence of hard labor as chattel. Opposing forces, primarily southern, protested. Immediately, they rolled back, mitigated, discounted and/or dismantled the denominational commitment to extirpate slavery. Six months later, the commitment to abolish slavery was quashed. William B. McClain noted in his book *Black People in the Methodist Church*, "The rules established at the Christmas Conference were to be applied only as far as they were consistent with the laws of the states in which the members resided."[2] The welcome mat for receiving Black folk into the Methodist Church during the eighteenth century turned out to be a slippery slope. No advocacy has interrupted that pattern for long. With Black folk in Methodism, the church has constantly taken a mighty step forward countermanded by two steps trudging "magnificently backward into the future."

When the Methodist Church retreated from its opposition to slavery, Black folk left and started their own, among them the African Methodist Episcopal Church, the African Methodist Zion Church, and the Colored Methodist Episcopal Church. Most of "those who stayed" lived on whatever came their way. Their status as half-slave and half-free remained.

What the gospel did or did not say about the enslavement of Black folk tore at the fabric of Methodism until it ripped apart during the 1844 General Conference. By marriage, Bishop James O. Andrew became a slave owner. His refusal to give them up or free them led to his suspension. Incensed over his suspension, the church split over the slavery question. Two denominations, one South and one North, remained divided for almost a century. In the meantime, African Americans who stayed in both communions continued to attend White churches. Eventually, they were encouraged to "do church as they saw fit" within the connection but under the aegis of White bishops until May 19, 1920. Bishop Robert Elijah Jones was elected as the first Black general superintendent in the Methodist Episcopal Church. Despite this reality, Black folk who stayed organized themselves into annual conferences and accomplished the work of ministry under circumstances some would label "separate but equal."

On May 10, 1939, the Methodist Episcopal Church, South; the Methodist Protestant Church; and the Methodist Episcopal Church united as the Methodist Church. Black folk belonging to nineteen separate conferences were placed in the Central Jurisdiction alongside five other jurisdictions. Separate but equal was codified. Under protest, the segregated jurisdiction continued until the merger of 1968. When the Central Jurisdiction died in 1968, Black Methodists for Church Renewal (BMCR) was created for the purpose of renewing the church as well as looking after the interests of the Black Church within the United Methodist denomination.

The lobbying efforts of National BMCR on behalf of the Black Church have been nothing short of amazing and a God-thing. God has used BMCR to help create the General Commission on Religion and Race, the Black Staff Forum, the Black College Fund, Ethnic Minority Local Church (EMLC) and its continuance in general agencies, Black Community Developers, and SBC21. In every instance, aspects of the church have realized the liberating effects of their particular ministry. General agencies and annual conferences have been challenged to "do the right thing" with regard to racial and ethnic minorities in hiring and firing practices as well as support. General agencies have made Ethnic Local Church (ELC) grants to churches and annual conferences as a way to empower and improve their ministry. Persons like me have benefited from the Black College Fund. Small colleges like my alma mater, Philander Smith College, have kept their doors open because of the Black College Fund. As a child of the Black Church, I know "God delivers me" is not a mantra. I have experienced it as a reality.

African Americans within The United Methodist Church have continued to dream, to hope, to envision a body of Christ unfettered by racism but truly comprised of all God's children. An excerpt of the vision statement writ large in the pages of a petition to the 1996 General Conference bears repeating word for word:

> Black people carry particular responsibilities for revitalizing and strengthening Black local churches within The United Methodist Church and offering our gifts to the wider church. Our prayer, which resounds through the decades and centuries past, is that as we take seriously our responsibility before God and in this United Methodist Church we will be joined by others. The denomination must also take seriously the need to support the endeavor, and in some places relinquish cultural and political control so that the work of renewal can be effective. The greater the contribution of the general church, the greater will be the renewal of the entire church's mission and ministry.[3]

Because of SBC21, local churches in the African American tradition are being strengthened all over the connection.

The Congregation Resource Center (CRC) and Partner Congregation (PC) model is at the heart of this renewal. When a local church demonstrates its desire and commitment to be strengthened, the SBC21 Coordinating Committee assigns it to a training event sponsored by one of the twenty CRCs. A team of five persons usually attends the event. In the best of all worlds, something cognitive, catalytic, and spiritual happens. And the team returns ready, willing, and able to help the church move to the next level. A rural congregation in South Carolina is one fitting example of the possibilities found in SBC21.

At the 2006 National BMCR meeting held in Dallas, Texas, the SBC21 Coordinating Committee asked that Rev. Marvin Taylor of Huger, South Carolina to share his story. He shared this scenario. The St. Thomas Charge—comprised of New Hope, Seward Chapel, and Zion United Methodist Churches—grew "from 567 to 1200 members in seven years." Taylor cited two training events sponsored by SBC21 as the reason. First, The New Life CRC in Jacksonville, Florida helped the St. Thomas Charge grasp the importance of stimulating church growth and being themselves in the worship context. Taylor commented further: "We were able to bring representatives from each of the churches. They came back and were able to help me share my vision concerning the importance of creating ministry for children, youth, young adults, and older adults. From the training the parishioners also understood the importance of being themselves in the worship experience." Second, on November 2005 Taylor and his team attended a training event sponsored by another CRC, St. Luke Community Church in Dallas, Texas. Because New Hope had grown from 267 members to 700 members, Zion from 190 to 240 members, Seward Chapel to 240 members, the St. Thomas Charge had to find some answers to its growth problems. Again, Rev. Taylor stated "this training helped us to create a model of leadership . . . to manage our growth . . . the St. Thomas Charge is one of SBC21's success stories." Without knowing it Rev. Taylor described the heart of the SBC21 enterprise. It is cognitive and catalytic, spiritual and spirit-driven. SBC21 is committed to and led by its overarching mantra: "Christ, Our Center for Hope, Healing and Wholeness." Last but not least, Pastor Taylor omitted another aspect of their success. The St. Thomas Charge has changed its status from a PC to a CRC. Now, SBC21 has begun sending churches to them for training.

The SBC21 model resident in the St. Thomas Charge and other Partner/CRC congregations is not just a model for the Black Church; it is for the whole church. Consequently, readers will find within these pages a panoramic view of SBC21 in terms of its history, its successes, its failures, and its future vision. Most of all, the book shows African American congregations taking greater responsibility for strengthening themselves and other congregations. That is the heart of the SBC21 story. Cooperation and support replace competition and fear. Hence, local churches, including their lay and clergy leadership, renew their strength for God's sake, not their own.

Whoever reads through the chapters of this book will not find simple solutions to complex problems vexing the Black Church or our denomination. Buried in the fiber of our mantra are the essentials to strengthen the life of any congregation. Look for them in our trials and errors, history, prayer, meditation, social activism, and personal witness—a witness in thought, word, and deed, communicating the power of a God who delivers and liberates the captive. And remember "Black folk who stayed" in the Methodist Church dare to stand up, "one more time," because God is not through with us yet; nor is God through with the whole church. Knowing that God has delivered us in the past, Black Methodists just can't shake the thought that "Our Time Under God Is Now."

NOTES

1. William B. McClain, *Black People in the Methodist Church* (Cambridge, MA: Schenkman Publishing Company, 1984), 57.

2. Ibid., 58.

3. Report on Strengthening the Black Church for the 21st Century," Report No. 3, (Petition Number: 21677-GJ-NonDis-OS; GCOM, 1996), 1996 General Conference (1997-2000), 583.

CHAPTER 1

A HISTORY OF BLACK METHODISM IN THE UNITED STATES

Youtha Hardman-Cromwell

BEGINNING WITH SLAVERY

What we know about Black preaching in the United States is that from its earliest practice there was a central focus: Freedom. But these exhortations on freedom had a two-pronged emphasis, freedom from sin and freedom from slavery. The SBC21 project notes the continuity of this approach to ministry and discipleship throughout the history of the Black Church. Black churches and their ministries continue to emphasize both a conversion from sin and release from the oppression, brutality, and dehumanization that continues as a result of American slavery and its legacy of racism.

John Wesley abhorred the practice of slavery. In a letter to William Wilberforce that was written in 1791, within a week of Wesley's death, he continued to speak out against this practice: "Go on, in the name of God and in the power of his might, till even American slavery (the vilest that ever saw the sun) shall vanish away before it."[1] Yet the issue of slavery and discrimination against persons of African heritage shaped and influenced Methodism development across its history in the United States.

Much occurred in the four centuries from the introduction by 1619 of African slaves into the United States, their introduction to Christianity, and the baptism of slaves by John Wesley in 1758 to the launching of the SBC21 initiative in The United Methodist Church at General Conference in 1992. Across this time period the issue of race, the place of those of African heritage has been central. Along the way were the emergence of several denominations from both splits and mergers, the creation of the Central Jurisdiction, and the establishment of the BMCR. Despite Methodism's ambivalence about its Black members, in his study of the Methodist Church published in 1953, Dwight Culver wrote, "The Methodist Church has more Negro members than the other 'white' denominations in the United States combined."[2] In 2004 over 420,000 African Americans were members of The United Methodist Church. They were six percent of the total United States membership.[3] Today Windsor Village UMC in Houston, Texas, a Black congregation, is the largest congregation in United Methodism. Its history reveals the way in which a congregation can be vital and also birth other vital congregations. Table 1.1 shows that there have always been African Americans in the Methodist Movement. But let's start at the beginning of the story.

When slaves arrived in the United States from the coasts of African countries, they brought with them religious traditions that included ancestor veneration and worship practices that embraced the use of music, dance, and spirited interaction. They had a regard for the sacred and for the work of the spirit in their communal and individual lives, an understanding of the power of prayer, and a strong identification with the centrality of community in giving meaning to individual existence.

When they encountered Christianity in the context of their enslavement, they had difficulty reconciling the presentation of Jesus as a messenger of God's love and concern for humanity with their inhuman treatment at the hands of those who professed to be disciples of this Jesus. Christianity taught equality and brotherhood and yet condoned the practice of tearing people from their homes and transporting them to a strange land to become slaves. "They did not have the superhuman capacity to reconcile in their own minds the contradictory character of the new religion."[4] Nevertheless, "the belief of John Wesley and the early preachers in the sacredness of all people, which lead [sic] to the rejections of slavery, and the spirited evangelistic appeal of Methodism in preaching and worship, were major factors in the attraction of slaves and free persons to The Methodist Church."[5] Unknown to many is the fact that in 1758 John Wesley baptized slaves, one a woman.[6]

TABLE 1.1 Comparisons of Black Membership in the Methodist Church

Year	Number of Blacks	Percentage of Total
1786	1890[a]	...
1790	12,000[b]	...
1797	12,215[a]	approximately 25
1816	42,000[c]	24.4
1840	87,197[d]	...
1861	200,000+[e]	...
1896	250,000-[b]	...
1900	239,274[f]	...

During the Life of the Central Jurisdiction
From General Minutes of The Methodist Church[g]

Year	Number of Blacks	Percentage of Total
1940	309,577	...
1944	282,654	...
1948	262,767	...
1952	273,358	
1955	359,786[h]	3.9
1956	352,972	...
1960	373,595	...
1964	373,595	...
1995	216,522*	39.2
2000	368,279*	22.5
2005	384,831*	20.8

The statistics in this table are from different sources. These sources are as follows:

[a]Russell E. Richey, *Early American Methodism*, 1991, 60.
[b]C. Eric Lincoln, and Lawrence H. Mamiya, *The Black Church in the African American Experience*, 1990, 65.
[c]Fergus M. Bordewich, *Bound for Canaan*, 2005, 87.
[d]Marilyn Magee Talbert, *The Past Matters*, 2005, 46.
[e]Ibid., 53.
[f]Ibid., 64.
[g]James S. Thomas, *Methodism's Racial Dilemma*, 1992, 151–153.
[h]The Lexington Conference, Central Jurisdiction. Philadelphia: Division of National Mission, 1957, 9.
*These figures from the General Board of Global Ministries are not regarded as reliable due to under-reporting and inconsistency.

SLAVES EMBRACE METHODISM

Methodism has always been biracial. Blacks were present at the first Methodist class meetings in America. When in 1762 Robert Strawbridge organized a class meeting of twelve persons in his home, among them was one known as "Aunt Annie," possibly a slave of the family.[7] Beatty, who was a Negro servant in the Heck household when Embury preached there, was a charter member of the John Street Methodist Society in 1779.[8] In 1828 Isabella Bomefree (Sojourner Truth) joined John Street also. Sojourner later became a member of the African Methodist Episcopal Zion Church.[9]

> From 1784, when African Americans were present and active in the earliest organization of The Methodist Episcopal Church, Black people were an integral part of Methodism in America. The sin of equivocation and racial separation were there also from the beginning. Despite the evil spirit of racial supremacy that flowed from many of the White people, and the ruthless processes of dehumanization and exploitation that were imposed over the centuries, Black people did not lose sight of the biblical vision of creation.[10]

White Methodists, such as John McKenney,[11] preached to Blacks and to Whites. A Northern minister, Nehemiah Adams, attended a number of Methodist prayer meetings and reported that "a white brother presided and read a portion of Scripture, but the slaves conducted the meeting."[12] Franklin calls ministering to Whites one of the unique services that Negro religious leaders rendered.[13]

The leadership of Blacks is well documented. They were preachers (exhorters) and missionaries. These included such persons as the better known Harry Hoosier, known as "Black Harry," who traveled with Bishop Francis Asbury. There was Henry Evans, a Virginia free-issue, who is credited with establishing Methodism in Fayetteville, North Carolina among both Blacks and Whites. However, the proscription laws of the twenties and thirties ended his preaching to Whites.[14] There was John Stewart who served among the Wyandotte Native Americans in Ohio. He "gave birth to the home missions' enterprise in the Methodist Church."[15] Richard Allen, who founded the African Methodist Episcopal church, was an adolescent convert to Methodism. After purchasing his freedom, he became an itinerant preacher and later returned to Philadelphia and St. George

Methodist Church.[16] In 1887 Emma Virginia Levi (later Brown) served the Church through the Woman's Home Missionary Society as a missionary. She was the matron at Browning House, an industrial home for girls in Camden, South Carolina. Other Black women who served these homes included Mrs. Marcus Dale, Mrs. Hester Williams, a former slave; and Mrs. Isabella Howells.[17]

The Mission Conference was the first structure in the Church to deal with the presence of Blacks. The 1824 General Conference approved Black preachers. Then in 1848 General Conference, responding to the need to provide for Black local congregations, approved separate annual conferences, and in 1864 African American Mission Conferences were authorized. John Wesley Church (now Tindley Temple) hosted the first such conference in Philadelphia in July 1864. It was not until the 1800s that Blacks were able to be fully ordained as elders. Finally in 1868 these Missionary Conferences were given the status of "Annual Conferences."[18]

Francis Burns was elected the first Black bishop of the Methodist Church North in 1858. In 1866 John W. Roberts was also elected. They both were elected to serve as missionary bishops in Africa.

> When they were a small, evangelical minority within the Church of England, the Methodists had vigorously denounced slavery as a travesty of divine, human, and natural justice.[19]

But that stance did not lead to full acceptance of Blacks in the American church. Franklin notes:

> After the [Revolutionary] War many churches accepted blacks, but whites were afraid that too liberal a policy would be disastrous to the effective control of slavery. Negro ministers and church officials, it was thought, would exercise too much authority over their slave communicants and would, perhaps, cause trouble on the plantations.[20]

This commitment to root out slavery, through the mid nineteenth century, was focused on personal "piety, discipline, and godly behavior — touching *both corporate and individual life* and certainly touching both slave and slaveholder."[21] Richey knows there was a lack of a public theology; not until the middle of the nineteenth century would their rhetoric include talk of making the nation Christian through educational, social, and political reforms.

Why did Black people become involved with the Methodist movement? *In Bound for Canaan*, Bordewich tells about a plot of a slave rebellion in Virginia, whose mastermind was a free blacksmith named Gabriel. The plan was to massacre all White persons except Quakers, Methodists, and Frenchmen.[22] It seems that the message of individual redemption that came in language even the uneducated could understand came to satisfy the spiritual thirst of the oppressed Blacks in both North and South. Even when the sentiment of the leadership of evangelicals shifted toward tolerance of slavery, individual preachers, including Methodists, continue to speak against slavery.[23] White Methodists were a part of the Underground Railroad. Calvin Fairbank was one of them. He was converted to be an abolitionist as a child while attending a Methodist revival, during which his family was housed in the home of two escaped slaves. He heard their story and later, as an adult, Fairbank served "the longest prison sentence on record for assisting a fugitive slave."[24]

Blacks accepted Methodism, but also transformed it. Through Black leaders such as Harry Hosier, Richard Allen, and Henry Evans, "Blacks nuanced Evangelicalism with African religious culture."[25]

The presence of Blacks in the Methodist movement met with various levels of acceptance and membership. Richey makes this astute observation:

> American Methodism derived from its southern beginnings a deep ambivalence about slavery and the Black. . . . Northern and Black historians have read this story as Methodist principle compromised and southern interest honored. . . . Both interpretations tend to locate the commitment to antislavery outside the South and to depict southerners as quite ready to embrace slavery. . . . However, such viewpoints . . . overlook the overwhelming southern character of the church during this early period and fail to recognize early antislavery as itself a southern impulse. They also fail therefore to appreciate the complexity of Methodist antislavery sentiment. It came laced with racism.[26]

Freeborn Garrettson is an example of this ambivalence. He was the circuit rider who summoned the scattered preachers to the historic Christmas Conference in Baltimore in 1784. He also had an epiphany, realized that slave-keeping was wrong, and released his slaves. It was his influence on Richard Allen's master that led to Allen and his brother being able to buy their freedom. He was the author of an antislavery tract, a preacher to Blacks, and developed a good, long-term, respectful relationship with

Richard Allen. Yet he failed to be egalitarian in his treatment of and sup-port of Black Methodists in general. He failed to give Harry Hoosier respect in his address to and treatment of him, preached in at least one instance in which Blacks had to stand outside to hear, promoted colonization as a way to keep the Blacks and Whites separate, regarded Blacks as primarily preferring servitude to Whites, and failed to use his position and author-ity to prevent the separation of Blacks who left the church with Richard Allen. When he attended the first annual conference of what became the African Methodist Episcopal Zion Church, he advised the Blacks to pro-ceed, expressing an expectation that at the next General Conference of the Methodist Episcopal Church a fully equal African Conference would be established. According to Ian Straker, it never was, and there is no ev-idence that Garrettson advocated for the Blacks in that legislative gath-ering.[27] Straker sums up Garrettson's ambivalence in this way:

> It is possible to discern in his writing a deep sympathy for slaveholders in a state of sin and mere pity for the plight of their slaves. In significant ways his own profound religious awakening did not move him to fully transcend his aristocratic, southern slaveholding heritage.[28]

Straker makes a further observation that captures the dynamic that shaped and, perhaps continues to shape, the dynamic between Black and White Methodists:

> The mixed and even conflicting views that African and white Methodist held of each other allowed for warm and friendly and supportive rela-tionships to exist despite the non-egalitarian views of African progress and civil rights held by Garrettson and others.[29]

Indeed, slavery and racism were key issues in the early church. In the Christmas Conference of 1784, a resolution passed against slavery, voting to expel from membership those who held slaves, but that resolve was sus-pended on behalf of the whole church in 1785 at a Conference in Balti-more.[30]

Those early days of Methodism were marked by "various impositions" that reflected the attitudes of many White Methodists. The report to the 1996 General Conference, "Report on Strengthening the Black Church for the 21st Century," lists some of these:

- White Bishops in the office of president over Black churches
- Assistance of Whites with the organization of separate Black missionary conferences (Methodist Episcopal Church and Methodist Protestant Church)
- Formation of the racially separated Colored Methodists Episcopal Church, formed by the Methodist Episcopal Church South for Black People[31]

SEPARATION: BLACKS AND WHITES

Ill-treatment began to lead to separations. Harding records one such voluntary separation:

> By the end of the War of 1812 the black Methodists in Charleston—the single largest black denomination—outnumbered the white membership ten to one. They had developed a quarterly conference of their own, and had custody of their own collections and control over the church trials of their own members. This independence was intolerable for the supervising white Methodists (and probably their non-Methodist friends as well). In 1815 they had acted against this black freedom, taking away privileges that they claimed were theirs to give, asserting that the African people had abused their freedom.[32]

The upshot of this was that the following year Morris Brown and other Black leaders went to Philadelphia, conferred with Richard Allen and others there, were ordained for pastorates in Charleston, and organized an independent African Association in 1817. After a dispute over burial grounds in 1818, more than 75 percent of the Black Methodists of Charleston withdrew from the White-dominated churches.[33]

The 1996 Strengthening the Black Church report notes:

> Black local churches were organized in the Methodist Episcopal Church. Their separateness signaled both the brokenness of the predominately White structures and the relative health of Black people who could affirm themselves, keep faith that change would come from God, and remain within the structures of predominantly White and decidedly hostile Methodist churches.[34]

In the beginning Blacks were worshipping in the same services and facilities with Whites. This was the case in both Southern and in Northern congregations. Various church histories give voice to these relationships between Black and White adherents to Methodism and the ways in which various Black congregations came into being. Some examples follow.

In its history, Georgetown's Dumbarton United Methodist Church, a descendent community of the first Methodist society in the District of Columbia, records this fact:

> Blacks, relegated to the balcony of the original Georgetown church, wanted their own place of worship. Henry Foxall, a slaveowner and prominent Georgetown Society member, helped make it possible. In 1816, he sold them his lot on Mill Street . . . and helped them build a small brick meetinghouse first known as "The Ark." . . . This church became Mount Zion Methodist Episcopal Church in 1844. By 1850, black Methodist Society members in Georgetown outnumbered whites 441 to 411. After years of preaching from white laypersons and pastors (provided by the Dumbarton Church until 1855), Mount Zion obtained its first black pastor in 1864.[35]

Mt. Zion United Methodist Church has continued to do ministry in Georgetown where few African Americans now reside. It sprang from the forty-seven Blacks in the Georgetown society in 1803.[36] In 2006 this congregation extended its ministry with a satellite ministry in Prince George's County, Maryland. That county has the largest concentration of African Americans of any of the suburbs of Washington, D.C.

Trinity United Methodist Church in Alexandria, Virginia records in its history that it emerged from a Methodist Society formed November 20, 1774, which later became the Alexandria Station Methodist Episcopal Church. In 1793, the first year that separate statistics were recorded, the congregation consisted of "58 white and 40 black." In 1832 Trinity helped to launch a Black church, Davis Chapel, which remained under Trinity's supervision until 1864. In 1956 it became Roberts Memorial Methodist Church. Roberts Memorial United Methodist Church continues in ministry on South Washington Street in Alexandria, Virginia.

In 1844 Trinity's minister, The Reverend Alfred Griffith, cosponsored a resolution at the General Conference that condemned slavery and led to the division of the Methodist Episcopal Church into northern and southern branches. Trinity remained a "northern church."[37] Trinity split in 1850 over the issue of slavery when its leaders took a strong stand against slavery. Washington Street Church of the Methodist Episcopal Church, South was formed by the 700 members who withdrew from Trinity.[38] In 1940 Trinity rejected merger with Washington Street and voted to move from its South Washington Street location to the western suburbs of Alexandria, moving its building brick by brick to the new location.[39]

Foundry United Methodist Church in Washington, D.C. is another congregation that began with Black members. It was established in 1814 with 38 members of whom 20 were European American and 18 were African American. Four years later there were 196 European American and 60 African American members.[40] During the first 20 years of its existence, Foundry began to treat its African American members as second-class citizens. When their requests for recognition within the church were denied, in 1835 the 279 African American members founded their own congregation, Asbury Methodist Episcopal, now Asbury UMC.[41] Asbury continues in ministry in downtown Washington, D.C. It has entered into a venture of partner ministry with Mt. Vernon Place UMC, formerly a part of The Methodist Episcopal Church South, and Wesley Theological Seminary to minister more fruitfully to the changing urban settings of these three Methodist institutions.

Another way in which racial discrimination shaped church life is exemplified in the history of Rohrerville UMC, Maryland. This congregation began its life as a United Brethren in Christ congregation in 1800 in Clopper Meeting House. When a second building became the church home, the Clopper Meeting House was turned over to the Negro slaves. "The white folks then occupied the gallery."[42]

One of the earliest African American Methodist congregations was established in 1791.[43] It began as "Society of Negro Adherents" in 1763 that was preached to by Ezekiel Cooper, a white man. In 1791 he said of them, "I had considerable satisfaction among them. . . . The dear black people seem to be alive to God having their hearts placed on things above."[44] In 1794 Rev. William Colbert, also White, noted that "the demeanor of the Oxon Hill blacks was a pleasant contrast to some of his trials and tribulations elsewhere."[45] His journal entry of January 23, 1794 included:

> Some years ago a few of these black people [at Oxon Hill] obtained their freedom and embraced religion, loved our society, built us a meeting house, and began to exhort people of their color to flee from the wrath, [sic] to come. God has blessed the labor in an extraordinary manner. Their society is very numerous and very orderly and to their great credit with pleasure I assert that I never found a white class so regular in giving

in their quarter age. As these poor people are, and the greater part are slaves, of whom never request anything. . . . They not only have their class meetings but also their days of examination in order to find out anything that may be amiss among them.[46]

Today it is St. Paul's UMC, which opened the Tanner Community Resource Center in 2000 to help fulfill and augment the church's outreach ministries, responding to "the changing needs of the society represented by the neighborhood" that St. Paul serves.[47]

Other Blacks pulled out from Methodist Churches to form their own formally independent and incorporated Methodist congregations; the first was Zoar in Philadelphia.

In 1787 Richard Allen led most of the black members out of St. George's Church and eventually into the new denomination, the African Methodist Episcopal Church. However, some African Americans remained in the St. George's Congregation."[48]

In 1794 three women and fifteen men of this remnant began holding separate worship services in homes, purchased property in Campington, north of Philadelphia's city limits in 1796, and built African Zoar Church. See figure 1.1. Zoar never severed its ties to the Methodist Episcopal Church and claims "Black Harry" Hosier as its "patron founding pastor." Francis Asbury, who preached there on several occasions, dedicated its first building and noted in his journal that at the August 4, 1796 service there was "an unwieldy congregation of white and black."[49] Zoar was not only active in seeking freedom from sin for Black people, but also freedom from oppression.

Zoar was actually more than just "active" in Philadelphia's Underground Railroad; it provided the movement its first home. . . . [M]embers choose the name Zoar, which means good will in Hebrew, because the church sought to provide a place of shelter to African American Methodists for worship. . . . A group of city residents, calling themselves the "Vigilant Committee," met in the church during the late 1830s, openly announced their intentions, and kept careful records of their efforts. Vigilance committees were devices used by abolitionists in the 1830s to help make it easier for escaped slaves to pass through the North. They claimed to exist to defend free blacks from kidnapping, but they really focused on assisting fugitives.[50]

Fig. 1.1. African Zoar Methodist Church, Center Building.
Reproduced by permission of The Library Company of Philadelphia.

Zoar was followed by Ezion in Wilmington, Delaware, and Sharp Street in Baltimore. Lincoln and Mamiya identify the independent church movement as "the first effective stride toward freedom by African Americans."

> Unlike most sectarian movements, the initial impetus for black spiritual and ecclesiastical independence was not grounded in religious doctrine or polity, but in the offensiveness of racial segregation in the churches and the alarming inconsistencies between the teachings and the expressions of the faith.[51]

Stith notes, for example, that it was not until the issue of Black bishops became present that the church addressed the issue of bishops being assigned to a resident area. Until then bishops were bishops of the whole church. On the occasion of the Central Jurisdiction reunion Bishop Forrest Stith says:

> They met together at conference meetings and decided which bishop would preside at each conference. After 1900, since the blacks were pressing in, church leaders decided to assign bishops to residential areas so they wouldn't have to have a black bishop.[52]

It was June 14, 1962 when the first integrated ordination service was held, pictured in figure 1.2.

NEGRO AND WHITE METHODIST bishops ordain a minister in what are believed to be the first such integrated service ever held in The Methodist Church. In the ordination Gary D. Harms of Great Bend, Kan., is one of the 15 Negro and white candidates ordained by Bishop Eugene Slater (second from left) of the Central Kansas Conference and Bishop Matthew Clair (third from left) of the Central West Conference of Negro congregations.

Fig. 1.2 First Integrated Ordination. "The Louisiana Methodist," June 14, 1962, page 10. Courtesy of General Commission on Archives and History, The United Methodist Church.

BLACK DENOMINATIONS EMERGE

Early in the history of Methodism racism led to the creation of three Black Methodist denominations that continue to be vital avenues for the nurture of African American Methodists and to be in mission for the cause of Christ: African Methodist Episcopal, African Methodist Episcopal Zion, and Colored (now Christian) Methodist Episcopal. See *Dark Salvation* by Harry B. Richardson and Appendix A for more information on these denominations.

The movement toward separation in worship of Black Methodists began to be widespread in 1786 when Blacks in Baltimore began gathering for prayer and devotions separately from White-controlled Methodist ministries. In that same year in Philadelphia, Pennsylvania Richard Allen organized 42 Blacks into a prayer meeting and society. Led by Richard Allen and Absalom Jones in 1791, a group of Blacks that had been asked to move during prayer left St. George Methodist Church. The first congregation, Bethel, remained under the Methodist Episcopal Church until 1814. Eventually in 1816 a Black Methodist denomination, African Methodist Episcopal Church was formed.[53] In 1916 there were 6000 churches, 5000 ministers, and 620,000 members.[54]

In 1796 in New York City a similar occurrence led to the creation of the African Methodist Episcopal Zion Church, under the leadership of

James Varick, Abraham Thompson, William Miller and others who belonged to John Street Methodist Church. Peter Williams, George Collins, and Christopher Rush were also in this group.[55] They left John Street, desiring to "be by themselves, exercising their own spiritual gifts and working to the benefit of their own people"[56] and built a church which they called Zion. Until 1920 The Methodist Episcopal Church supplied this congregation with ordained preachers. When their request for Black ordained ministers was denied, the congregation moved to form its own denomination in New York City. It began with 6 churches, 19 preachers, and 1,426 members. In 1930 there were 2,466 local churches.[57]

Other factions of Methodism also emerged that served the Black population in the United States. The 1913 *Methodist Yearbook* records their existence:

- Union American Methodist Episcopal Church was founded in 1805 by Rev. Peter Spencer, who was a member of Asbury Methodist Episcopal Church in Wilmington, Delaware. In that year 41 of Asbury's members were Black. They desired certain rights that were denied to them and withdrew, with no intention of forming a new denomination, to what was then Zion Methodist Episcopal. Again their desire to have a voice "in selecting their ministry" led Spencer and his followers to withdraw in 1812 and in 1813 to incorporate as the Union Church of Africans. Peter Spencer organized 31 churches, each with a school house. In 1846 a division occurred resulting in the African Union Church and the Union American Methodist Episcopal Church. In 1930 this denomination had 75 churches, 148 ministers, and 10,169 members.[58] In 1916 it had 212 churches, 170 ministers, and 19,000 members.[59]
- African Union Methodist Protestant Church with nine congregations united in 1865 with fourteen congregations of a Methodist society known as the First Colored Methodist Protestant Church. In 1916 there were 125 churches, 200 ministers, and 4000 members.[60]
- Colored Methodist Protestant Church was formed in 1840 when 100 members of Black Methodist churches in Maryland and adjoining States met and organized in Elkton, Cecil County, Maryland. Their organization reflected that of the Methodist Protestant Church which had organized a few years before. They adopted the book of discipline of The Methodist Episcopal Church and the polity of the Methodist Protestant Church that did not include the episcopacy. By 1926 they had declined to 3 churches with 533 members from 26 churches with 1,967 in 1916.[61]
- Reformed Zion Union Apostolic Church was formed at the close of the Civil War in 1869 in southeastern Virginia by Rev. James R. How-

ell who was a minister in the African Methodist Episcopal Zion Church, first taking the name Zion Union Apostolic Church. The people reacted to the fact that they were not permitted to gather in the white churches for worship, they had no educated ministry, and "they were not in sympathy with the other Negro denominations." Rev. Howell organized them.[62] They disorganized a few years later. Then in 1881 Rev. John M. Bishop gathered the scattered members and organized under the name Reformed Zion Union Apostolic Church.[63] By 1906 there were 45 churches, 33 ministers, and 3,059 members.[64] By 1930 there were 48 churches and 4,538 members chiefly in Virginia and North Carolina.[65]

- Reformed Methodist Union Episcopal Church came out of the African Methodist Episcopal Church and organized in 1885 as the Independent Methodist Church among representatives of congregations in South Carolina and Georgia. They disagreed about the election of ministerial delegates to the General Conference. In 1916 they adopted the polity of the Methodist Episcopal Church.[66] In 1896 it decided to create an episcopacy and change the name to Reformed Methodist Union Episcopal Church. In 1916 there were 58 churches, 72 ministers, and 4,397 members.[67]

- The Independent African Methodist Episcopal Church resulted from a meeting in 1897 in Jacksonville, Florida of eight pastors of the African Methodist Episcopal Church (AME). They discussed their disagreement with AME church administration. They decided to withdraw and form this new denomination. In 1900 another disagreement with AME's resulted in the Independent African Methodist Episcopal Church at Coldwater, Mississippi. The two groups remained separate until 1919. In 1930 there were 29 churches and 1003 members.[68]

White Methodists were prominent in the 1830s and 1840s among abolitionists who worked unsuccessfully to end slavery in the United States. Among them were Orange Scott, Lucious Matlock, Abel Stevens, and Wilbur Fisk.

> Finally, by 1842 [Orange Scott] gave up hope that the Methodist Church would ever end its deep investment in slavery. He then left the church and led himself and others into a new Church: The Wesleyan Methodist Connection.[69]

The power of the proslavery advocates in the church was too strong during the late 1700s and first three decades of the nineteenth century. By the mid 1800s the Methodist Episcopal Church actively opposed antislavery groups. "The church began to bring to trial those ministries who identified themselves as abolitionists or promoted antislavery ideas."[70] Conferences that took such action were Ohio, Baltimore, New York, Philadelphia, Pittsburg, and Michigan.

When slavery became a dividing issue in 1844, the Methodist Episcopal Church split into two units: The Methodist Episcopal Church (North)[71] and The Methodist Episcopal Church South. In 1864 the Methodist Church (North) created Negro Mission Conferences. The first was the Delaware Conference and then came the Washington Conference. In 1866 the Northern Methodists formed the Freedman's Aid Society, which created a number of schools, institutions, and programs for freed slaves. In all, twelve colleges were founded, including Bennett College, Bethune-Cookman College, Clark University, Dillard University, Meharry Medical School (which met first in the basement of Clark Memorial Methodist Episcopal Church), and Gammon Theological Seminary (now associated with the Interdenominational Theological Center in Atlanta).[72] Then in 1880 it established the Woman's Home Missionary Society whose primary objective was to create schools and institutions in the south for former slaves.[73]

Out of this north/south split arouse the Colored Methodist Episcopal Church, which set aside the African Americans in The Methodist Episcopal Church South to separate them—involuntarily —from its White constituents. *The Methodist Yearbook, 1916* describes the situation in this way:

> To meet the new condition brought on by emancipation, The General Conference of 1866 of the Methodist Episcopal Church, South, made careful provision for their colored members by adoption of two reports. As a result of their action five Annual Conferences were organized, and on December 25, 1870, they were set apart at Jackson, Tenn., as a distinct ecclesiastical body. They began with two bishops, a few preachers and members; no schools, but little church property, no leaders of experience and no money.[74]

At the beginning of the Civil War there were about 270,000 Black members of the Methodist Church, South. At the end of the War, there were 78,742 remaining because a large number of them had joined the African Methodist Episcopal Church, the African Methodist Zion Church, and other Black Methodist church bodies. In 1916 there were 3,196 churches, 3,072 ministers, and 240,798 members.[75] By 1930 there were 2,518 churches with 202,713 members.[76]

An understanding of this early history of relationships among Black and White Methodists, without an understanding of how "slavery and segregation formed the thinking and feelings of White Americans before the separate racial jurisdictions actually became a fact,[77] is important to understand the creation and elimination of what came next: The Central Jurisdiction.

THE CENTRAL JURISDICTION

With the reunion of the Northern and Southern Methodist, joined with the Methodist Protestant Church in 1939, the Blacks were set apart into The Central Jurisdiction to satisfy the prejudices of the South. This was a unique jurisdiction since, unlike the others, it was racially based rather than geographically determined. Although there were other issues none of them rose to the importance of the question of what to do with the Black members.

> During the negotiations leading to union [of the Methodist Church North and South with the Protestant Methodist], several proposals were set forth, but all of the major ones recommended either a separate racial structure or an all-African American Methodist Church which the then-members of the church would be asked to join voluntarily. Just as slavery had been the determining factor in Methodist relations with African Americans, so also segregation had determined these relations during discussion on union.[78]

At the Uniting General Conference this plan to involuntarily separate the Black members into the separate Central Jurisdiction passed by a vote of 135 to 15,[79] and the General Conferences of the three denominations all adopted this plan by substantial margins. Only the annual conference of North Mississippi failed to accept the plan by a majority vote.[80]

> For the first time in the Methodist Episcopal Church history there was an official policy of segregation. While the plan made provisions for the black membership to have equal jurisdictional participation in the national denomination's General Conference, General Boards, Council of Bishops and so on, and gave to the black membership the right to elect its own leadership and establish its own policies and procedures; the Methodist Church was, by the same token, establishing a policy of dealing with its black membership on the basis of race. They were to be segregated at every connectional level of the church's life below that of its national structure.[81]

The African American delegates to the General Conference did not support the plan; several leaders spoke out against it even before 1939. One was a young pastor, Rev. Charles Carrington who said that the plan not only violated the principles of brotherhood in organization of believers into the Church, but also their dominance in the life and teachings of Jesus.[82] In the Northern Church there was a rich history of Blacks that could not be overlooked, but the Joint Commission working on the plan, sought to devise one that would not offend the sensibilities of the Southern Church while adhering "to the North's historic mission to blacks."[83] Barbara Brown sums up its impact well:

> The creation of the Central Jurisdiction was one of the most historic detours in Methodist annals—one that delayed the church's march toward integration and sullied the church's reputation for more than a century.[84]

McClain summarizes the various reactions of Blacks:

> There were a few black Methodists who tried to offer what they considered to be moderating or perhaps pragmatic comments suggesting that the Central Jurisdiction would create equal opportunities and powers with the white Jurisdictions. A few others favored it because they saw it as a greater chance in obtaining status in prestigious positions and in exercising leadership for the race under the auspices of The Methodist Church. And a very few favored saving the church embarrassment and withdrawing from the church.[85]

Daniel Shaw expressed that unpopular view, expressing the view that the Blacks were a hindrance to the Whites and vice versa.

There were three large groups of Black Methodists at the end of the Uniting Conference:

1. Those who had remained with the northern branch, and were included in the nineteen Annual Conferences that became the Central Jurisdiction (See table 1.2)
2. Those in the Methodist Episcopal and Methodist Episcopal Zion Churches
3. Those in the Colored Methodist Episcopal church who separated from the southern branch in 1870[86]

There was no mass exodus from the Methodist Church. Why did the Blacks stay and participate in the Church through the Central Jurisdiction in the face of the taunts from other Black churches that they were a part of a "Jim Crow" church?[87] They believed that their presence was important. Thomas cites two reasons:

1. An "instinctive conviction" that the Church's historic connection

with Black people represented a basic intention to build brotherhood among all persons and that the membership of Blacks would help to achieve this goal.

2. The vigor of the Church's outreach to Blacks, beginning in slavery and continuing in the building of schools for the freedmen after the Civil War.[88]

The first Central Jurisdiction Conference was held in June 1940 at Union Memorial Methodist Church in St. Louis. It reported a membership of 344,671. Its major business was the election of bishops; W. A. Hughes, who died within a month of his election, and Lorenzo Houston King, who was a member of the New York Conference and did not belong to the Central Jurisdiction, were elected, joining Bishop Robert E. Jones, who had been elected by the General Conference of 1920. These three had the tasks of administering a racially close-knit unit that was geographically dispersed and sociologically diverse.[89] See table 1.2 for a list of the Central Jurisdiction Conference and figure 1.3 for a map of their locations.

The Central Jurisdiction immediately moved to serve Black Methodists through efforts "to enrich worship experiences, upgrade church parsonages and church facilities, recruit and train more lay and clergy leaders, increase and enliven the work of women's groups."[90] Figure 1.4 pictures two of these activities. The national church supported these efforts. For various reasons at the same time there was in the Central Jurisdiction, and among some in the wider Church, a commitment to agitating and keeping up pressure for its elimination.

Fig. 1.3 Map of the Boundaries of Central Jurisdiction Conferences. Oliver S. Baketel, *The Methodist Yearbook*, 1914, 28. Dark solid lines represent conference boundaries. Broken lines represent state boundaries or other divisions.

Fig. 1.4. Pastors School, 1951. Teachers and Students of Washington Conference School of Missions (second series) at Ebenezer Church and Giddings School, Washington, D.C. June 27-July 2, 1944, Fannie D. Tyler, Dean. Courtesy of General Commission on Archives and History, The United Methodist Church. Photo by Oscar.

TABLE 1.2 Central Jurisdiction Conferences	
1939–1960	1960–1968
Atlantic Coast Area Central Alabama Florida Georgia South Carolina **Baltimore Area** Delaware Washington East Tennessee North Carolina **New Orleans Area** Louisiana Mississippi Texas Upper Mississippi West Texas **St. Louis Area** Central West Lexington Southwest Tennessee	**Atlantic Coast Area** Florida Georgia South Carolina **Baltimore Area** Delaware North Carolina Washington **Nashville-Birmingham Area** Central Alabama East Tennessee Mississippi Tennessee Upper Mississippi **New Orleans Area** Louisiana Texas West Texas **St. Louis Area** Central West Lexington Southwest

Lists of Annual Conferences of the Central Jurisdiction, 1939 to 1968. The United Methodist Church, archives, Pamela Cosby, 2004.

After seventeen years, the process to eliminate the Central Jurisdiction began when the 1956 General Conference amended The Constitution with Article IX. This change promised the opportunity for churches transfer, including those in the Central Jurisdiction to transfer to geographic jurisdictions; this would be one way out of the dilemma that the Central

Jurisdiction had created. By the 1960 General Conference when the Commission on Interjurisdictional Relations made its report, only about one percent of the churches in the Central Jurisdiction had transferred. This transfer process really began in 1964 and took almost ten years to complete. See table 1.3.

TABLE 1.3 Central Jurisdiction Merger Dates	
Central Jurisdiction Conference	**Year Merged**
Delaware, Lexington, Washington, DC.	1964
Central West	1965
Tennessee-Kentucky, North Carolina, Virginia	1968
Florida	1969
Gulf Coast (Texas), West Texas	1970
Louisiana	1971
Georgia, South Carolina, Southwest	1972
Central Alabama, Upper Mississippi, Mississippi	1973

This table reflects the dates when Central Jurisdiction Conferences merged with Geographic Conferences, The United Methodist Church. General Minutes of the United Methodist Church 1964–1974 (Thomas, 1992, 132).

The 1960 Central Jurisdiction Conference had set up a committee of five to study the Central Jurisdiction in an effort to continue the process of abolishing the Central Jurisdiction. James S. Thomas was to convene the group.

> Understanding its mission to be both working with other committees or commissions and developing its own plans, the Central Jurisdiction Study Committee began a series of meetings and consultations in various sections of the Jurisdiction. The Committee met with the African American members of the Commission on Interjurisdictional Relations, with the College of Bishops of the Central Jurisdiction, and with many persons and groups who wanted to know the point of view of the Central Jurisdiction's leaders.[91]

This exploration resulted in an exploratory meeting in Cincinnati in 1962 to seek a common mind. One result was a realignment of the annual conferences of the Central Jurisdiction so that each one would be within the boundaries of one regional jurisdiction. See table 1.2. Figure 1.5 shows the Committee of Five proposed reorganization.

The Committee of Five also prepared a series of petitions for the 1964 General Conference "to provide a way by which the high ideals of The Methodist Church could be expressed in its *Book of Discipline*."[92] They stated the following:

> The abolition of the racially segregated Central Jurisdiction of The Methodist Church is not an end in itself. Removal of this unit from the organizational structure of the church is of real significance only as this action will clearly promote a truly inclusive Methodist fellowship.[93]

It was at the 1964 General Conference that the Commission on Inter-jurisdictional Relations made a report calling for the elimination of the Central Jurisdiction without a specific plan to transfer its conferences into the regional Jurisdictions.[94] The lack of a plan was not acceptable to the Central Jurisdiction's representatives. The Committee of Five had developed such a plan, which had been adopted by the Central Jurisdictional Conference.

Heavy lines represent boundaries of regional jurisdictions. Light lines represent boundaries of proposed Central Jurisdiction annual conferences.

Figure 1.5. Map of Proposed Annual Conferences in Relation to Regional Jurisdictions
Source: "Study Document on Realignment of the Central Jurisdiction to the 1964 General Conference," The Committee of Five, Insert. Courtesy of General Commission on Archives and History, The United Methodist Church

At this same General Conference, liberal Whites, embarrassed by the failure of the denomination to eliminate the Central Jurisdiction, led a kneel-in to stir consciences. It was also this Conference that elected two African Americans to the episcopacy to serve integrated jurisdictions: Bishop Prince A. Taylor of New Jersey and Bishop James S. Thomas of Iowa.[96] Note that in 1967 Bishop L. Scott Allen was the last bishop elected by the Central Jurisdiction, making a total of 14 Black bishops.

In adopting the Plan of Union with the Evangelical United Brethren Church there was no provision for the Central Jurisdiction. "In 1966, The Methodist Church, after much agony, pressure, and a combination of many events and factors (including merger with the Evangelical United Brethren Church) set a date for termination of the Central Jurisdiction."[97] McClain notes that the Central Jurisdiction had died a slow death. But it did not mean the death of racial issues in the Methodist Church.

> Deliberate removal of the racial jurisdiction from the legal structures of The United Methodist Church moved in the direction that most United Methodists—Black and White—believed fulfilled God's plan for this denomination of the institutionalized church.[98]

Its history made the need for change in many aspects of the life and work of the Methodist church, particularly in the area of race relations evident. Brown notes:

> Grant S. Shockley describes [1968] as a "pivotal year" for Methodism regarding inclusiveness: "The events of that year were to have continuing effects on what black Methodists were to think and feel and how they were to define their faith, themselves, and how they would live their lives as United Methodist."[99]

Bishop Thomas reflecting on the elimination of the Central Jurisdiction observed that, "It is easier to remove a racial structure than it is to overcome the social forces that caused the structure in the first place." Gil Caldwell, notes in his United Methodist News Service Commentary:

> To assume that, because the structure has been removed, the social forces that caused the structure have also been removed, is to engage in an act of denial that subsequent generations will have to face because we did not.... [I]f we believe that the significant presence of African Americans

at every level of the church means that racially insensitive, sometimes racist, social forces have been overcome, we do not appreciate the contemporary accuracy of these words of Bishop Thomas.[100]

BIRTH OF BLACK METHODISTS FOR CHURCH RENEWAL

To address the ongoing concerns of Blacks in The United Methodist Church, a new organization emerged in 1968: Black Methodists for Church Renewal. Although technically the elimination of the Central Jurisdiction offered Blacks the opportunity to participate fully in the life of the Church at all levels of the connection, "*de facto* inclusiveness has not yet occurred."[101] One of the benefits of the Central Jurisdiction was that it had provided Blacks opportunity to use and develop leadership and administrative skills that prepared them to carry out the tasks of the Central Jurisdiction and to fully participate in the new denomination, given or gaining the opportunity to do so.

> Black people, though anguished and tired, chose to endure the Central Jurisdiction, indeed appreciated some aspects of the autonomy that went with it, and hoped that God would make the change that would open the Methodist Church to new possibilities for justice, equality, and unity.[102]

BMCR provided the vehicle for gathering and working in a caucus with the hope of developing "a life of power and unity in the new United Methodist Church."[103] The goal was to provide a forum for Black Methodists, giving them the opportunity to define issues and develop strategies to deal with those issues that would bring about changes in The United Methodist Church. The vision was that these changes would empower Black Methodists at all levels of the church, including all of its agencies and related institutions.

> BMCR's lobbying efforts have given birth to the General Commission on Religion and Race [1968], the Ethnic Minority Local Church, the Black Staff Forum, and Strengthening the Black Church for the 21st Century" (SBC21) [1996].[104]

In 1984 in a major undertaking BMCR held its Black Church Growth Consultation in Atlanta where teams of congregations received intensive training.[105] (Figure 1.6 pictures examples of the programs and events that BMCR continues to offer to develop the spiritual lives and ministry capabilities of the Black Church.) BMCR names two of the 23 persons who make up SBC21 Committee. Through its Executive Director, currently Cheryl Walker, BMCR has helped identify both churches and resources for its work.[106]

Figure 1.6. Training and Youth Events in 1984 at BMCR Event, Atlanta, Georgia. Courtesy of General Commission on Archives and History, The United Methodist Church.

The website of The General Commission on Religion and Race lists the purpose of this caucus of Black members of The United Methodist Church:

- To empower and involve Black Methodists for effective witness and service among pastors, laity in local churches, conferences and schools, and the larger community.

- To encourage and involve Black Methodists and others in the struggle for economic and social justice.
- To expose latent and overt forms of racism in all local, regional, and national agencies and institutions of The United Methodist Church.
- To act as an agitating conscience on all boards and agencies of The United Methodist Church in order to keep them sensitive to the needs and expressions of a "genuinely" inclusive and relevant church.
- To keep before the church the crucial issues facing us by initiating action and supporting church agencies which realistically deal with the needs of Black people; i.e., issues spelled out in "The Findings of Black Methodists for Church Renewal" and the other occasional documents adopted by Black Methodists for Church Renewal, Inc.
- To initiate, develop and implement strategies and instruments for the development, the maintenance, and the growth of strong black local churches.
- To provide an instrument through which we can educate and cultivate the black constituency of our church toward a greater knowledge of Africa and the Caribbean and our mission there; to facilitate dialogue between blacks in The United Methodist Church and African and Caribbean Christians; and to provide more black input, awareness and sensitivity in the policy-making procedures of the Board of Global Ministries as it relates to Africa, the Caribbean, and other boards and agencies as they relate to the black church.[107]

The Black Methodists who had remained in The Methodist Church had been patient, though not passive, for over 200 years.[108] Black Methodists were hopeful, knowing full well that racist forces remained in The Methodist Church.

Black Methodists for Church Renewal held out great hope, but knew well that the racist forces of evil that remained in the new United Methodist Church and the society and culture at large, were not dead, nor were they truly interested in renewal for racial justice and "inclusiveness." Much of what was accomplished in the arenas of Episcopal leadership and general church structures was negated in annual conferences and local churches.[109]

BMCR's assertion that "our time under God is now" was an expression of both hope and recognition that the struggle was not ending in 1968. It was an unequivocal claim of both anger and forbearance made by those who had remained within the structures of The United Methodist Church, spiritual descendents of those of African heritage who had been in the Methodist societies, and congregations from the beginnings of Methodism on this continent. When BMCR (the National Conference of Negro Methodists as it began)[110] first met in February 1968 in Cincinnati, James M. Lawson, Jr. identified the questions before them: "Where are we in The Methodist Church today? What do we want for the whole Church? How do we move in that direction?" These questions remain the continuing focus of BMCR.[111] Barbara Thompson, then General Secretary of the General Commission on Religion and Race, identified BMCR's gift to the church in this way: "BMCR's continual holding forth of the manifestations of racism within the Church is evidence of the caucus's [sic] loving belief that renewal of the Church is possible."[112]

STRENGTHENING THE BLACK CHURCH FOR THE 21ST CENTURY

The 1976 General Conference established a missional priority to strengthen the ethnic minority church.[113] At that time the term "ethnic" was primarily understood to be "Blacks," but as this missional priority continued in other quadrennial, the term expanded to include other persons of color.

Another African American effort to promote the inclusive nature of The United Methodist Church must be noted. In 1980 a group of African American United Methodists, feeling the need to bring "songs of the soul and soil" to the wider church, gathered the songs and published *Songs of Zion* through the United Methodist Publishing House and Abingdon Press.

The 1966 *Methodist Book of Hymns* included only one hymn, "Stand by Me" by African American composer Charles Tindley. Also five Negro spirituals were included. *Songs of Zion* brought to predominantly White congregations "sacred music of African-American culture." Many of those songs were included in the 1989 hymnal, the latest edition. William McClain, who laid the groundwork for *Songs of Zion*, on the occasion of its 25th anniversary stated that he "believes the effect of the songbook on the church have [sic] been significant, reaching across racial and denominational boundaries."[114]

The emergence of women as clergy leaders must be mentioned. In 1926 Laura Lange of the Lexington Conference was the first Black woman to be ordained deacon in the Methodist Episcopal Church.[115] Sallie Crenshaw was the first Black woman ordained elder and "admitted into full connection in an annual conference of the Methodist Church" in 1958.[116] It was 1984 when the first Black woman was elected bishop.[117] This was Leontyne E. C. Kelly, who had to leave the Southeastern Jurisdiction Conference were she was a candidate to be elected in the Western Jurisdiction. But it wasn't until 1992 that the first Black woman, J. Jeannette Cooper, a member of West Ohio Conference, was appointed District Superintendent.[118]

When the twenty-first century was about to dawn, Black United Methodists continued to be ever more aware that "our time under God is now." Across the church in recent years congregations had decreased in size and in the number of congregations that were part of the United Methodist connection.

> At a more fundamental level, the church really lives out its life of faith, witness, and service at the local level, in the community, where relations are more personal, communal, and voluntary. Methodists are not a structure, they are the people who join local churches, gather for worship, live in communities and act out their faith in the society.[119]

What was happening at the local church level was a serious concern across the connection. Questions aroused around what makes a congregation vital, what promotes church growth, what contributes to stagnation and apathy in congregants and congregations. There were Black congregations that could be identified as growing, active, and passionate in worship and service. In addition, Black congregations were noted for a higher percentage of attendance by its membership. What could those congregations that were experiencing a decline or stagnation do to join the congregations that seemed to be more alive and vital?

A Plan of Action was presented to the General Conference to create Black United Methodist Congregation Resource Centers in the Black Church to meet the challenges of being in ministry in the twenty-first century. The 1996 report states the vision in this way:

> As we take account of the demand that God places upon our lives, we are compelled to remember that increased memberships, larger attendance, and more financial gifts alone are not enough to indicate strength and vitality. In addition, we will need to be able to declare that we catch a glimpse of growing unity and community; we will need spiritual depth expressing itself not only in gathered worship but also in the broad aspects of our physical and material existence; we will need wholeness and wholesomeness of personal and community life that finds increasing expression in everyday relationships; and we will need to center our response in Christ so that our lives will receive the gift of His transforming power, and our being and doing in church, community, nation and world will bespeak the glory of God.[120]

African Americans have a proud heritage as Methodists dating back almost 250 years to the beginning of the Methodist Movement. The histories of several local congregations will demonstrate this fact, lay bare their vicissitudes, and lay out the variety of paths that these congregations have taken to the twenty-first century.

One of the churches that emerged in these centuries and continues to minister today is St. Mark UMC in Chicago. It was born in 1893 when Rev. S. C. Gooseley was sent there to organize among Blacks a Methodist Church. St. Mark United Methodist Church came into existence in an organizational gathering in the home of John and Flora Washington. Others present were Henry and Nellie Bomar, Mr. and Mrs. Richard Moore, Mr. and Mrs. Richard Jones, and George Jackson. Their first church home was a fire-damaged building that was owned by a White congregation. The new congregation repaired the church "to such a state that the white congregation reclaimed the property."[121] At that time there was no recourse for the St. Mark members. Since that time St. Mark has had three church homes: figure 1.7 shows two of these.

Fig. 1.7. Top: The Store where St. Mark first met; Center: Its facility at 50th and Wabash; Bottom: An early dressmaking class sponsored at St. Mark. Source: Courtesy of General Commission on Archives and History, The United Methodist Church.

Between 1923 and 1937 St. Mark's membership increased from 2,200 to 4,412 persons. Between 1940 and 1952 the Sunday School grew to over a thousand members.

St. Mark takes pride in the ministers that have served it, claiming a history of "great preachers."[122] These include pastors who

- led them out of debt and to expand and upgrade its facilities (Rev. J. W. Robinson, Dr. Damon P. Young, and Rev. Charles Wesley Jordan);
- helped them increase their membership (Rev. John B. Redmond) and to more fully participate in the life of the church (Rev. Samuel Sweeney, Rev. Matthew W. Clair, and Rev. Harry B. Gibson);
- were appointed district superintendent (Rev. Matthew W. Clair, Jr.) and bishops (Bishop Matthew W. Clair, Jr. and Bishop Charles Wesley Jordan);
- were elected president of National Black Methodist for Church Renewal (Rev. Dr. Maceo D. Pembroke);
- became a president of St. Paul School of Theology (Rev. Dr. Myron McCoy).

Under Rev. Charles Wesley Jordan the St. Mark housing for senior citizens was completed.[123] In January 2004 Rev. Dr. Jon E. McCoy was appointed senior pastor. He "has initiated many new innovative ministries to serve the quickly and constantly changing present age, while preserving many meaningful St. Mark traditions."[124]

St. Mark also takes pride in its strong lay leadership, its establishment of other congregations, its growing music department, its outstanding United Methodist Women and Men's organizations, and its outreach to the community. This outreach includes Girl and Boy Scouts and physical and spiritual feeding. But is also includes a credit union and programs to assist in employment and with veterans affairs. It continues to be a predominantly African American congregation.

In its conclusion St. Mark's history includes this telling notation: "To become full participating members of this church – it took us from 1784 to 1964 – 180 years."[125] St. Mark stated in its application that its goal is to bring to its role as a SBC21 resource center this history and its current ministry through which it hopes to provide inspiring worship that engages individuals and families and provides them the opportunity to experience the presence of Christ, and to participate in ministries of witness and outreach while reflecting both traditional worship practices and incorporating contemporary worship elements.

Another early church that has participated in SBC21 is Brooks Memorial UMC in Jamaica Heights, New York. It is an African American congregation that has a shorter history than St. Mark, but it also brings its heritage and current ministry to the table to share in helping other congregations rise to the challenge of ministry in the twenty-first century. It began in ministry in 1924.

> Humble, modest, capable, Richard A. McCarthy laid a solid foundation for growth. Famed for his conviction that the church should minister to social as well as purely spiritual needs, the present day Brooks Memorial in its broad social, recreational and cultural program is a fulfillment of a dream of the Founder and advanced through the years by loyal members and friends.[126]

Rev. McCarthy and his family were among the first Black settlers in Queens, having moved there in 1916 to an area without electricity and with public transportation that was limited to trolley car lines and elevated trains that stopped at the city line between Brooklyn and Queens.

Starting with a prayer group of persons from various denominations in his home, a nucleus of a neighborhood church formed. With the group's increase, in 1924 he was asked to organize a mission. Rev. McCarthy had been a faithful member and class leader at St. Marks Methodist Church in Manhattan. The congregation and pastor, Rev. John Robinson, along with Rev. Richard Frances from Maspeth Methodist Church, supported his mission. When the new congregation obtained its own place of worship, it was named for Dr. William H. Brooks who had become renowned and respected as St. Marks pastor from 1897 to 1923.

> The known Charter members were: The McCarthy family, Lucy and Yeadon Ready, Floyd, Mary and Herbert Jefferson, Lucille White, George Wheeler Sr., Harrison and Jessie Holmes, Eva and Harry Singleton, Veora Harris, Marie Evans, James and Malvina Goodwin, Henry and Mabel James.[127]

In 1930 the church was received into the Delaware Conference of the Methodist Episcopal Church with a membership of 123.[128] Having refused salary for the duration of his service, Rev. McCarthy led the congregation until 1939.

Rev. Charles L. Carrington led the congregation, beginning in 1941. During his "spiritual, inspirational, civic-minded leadership"[129] the membership doubled as persons rallied around this youthful pastor. The membership reached 1,500 in the years after World War II. Today it is a strong middle class congregation of about five hundred persons.

Brooks Memorial celebrates several firsts:

- Florence V. Lucas, who had been a member of Brooks since she was 14, became the first African American woman to pass the bar examination and to be admitted to practice law in Queens.[130] In 1996 she was honored by Brooks for several firsts, including being elected to highest court in Methodism.[131]
- Rev. Lillian Pope, who was the first woman ordained as a deacon in the Delaware Conference, was assigned as Director of Religious Education from 1944 to 1950.[132]
- In 1949 the church hosted a dinner to celebrate the appointment of the first African American Queens District Attorney, Westervelt Taylor.[133]
- In 1964, the pastor, Rev. Carrington became the first Executive Secretary of the Board of Missions and Church Extension of the New York Conference of the Methodist Church.[134]

In 1954 Brooks was selected "as one of the five outstanding residential Methodist Churches in the nation, and was featured for study at the Washington D.C., National Convention on Urban Church Life."[135] Then in 1956:

> A historic event occurred which was to have far-reaching effects. The Bishops' Conference on Brotherhood was held at Brooks. Bishop Love of the Baltimore Area of the Delaware Conference and Bishop Frederick B. Newell of the New York State area led the discussion about integration of the Methodist Church.[136]

This was followed in 1963 by the congregation joining a church-sponsored protest rally to demand more construction jobs for African Americans.

In 1964 Brooks left the segregated Central Jurisdiction and transferred into the New York Area of the Northeastern Jurisdiction of The Methodist Church as a result of much hard work by Rev. Carrington. This year also saw the initiation of a yearlong emphasis on expanding and strengthening youth programming.[137] The following year the first Summer Day Camp served 1,536 children and 250 high school and college students were provided summer jobs.[138]

In 1974 Sunday worship times were changed to 8 and 10:30 a.m.[139] The decade from 1984 to 1994 included the initiation of a five-day a week Senior Center, establishment of a Rites of Passage Program for both males and females, and a flourishing new program, Mentoring Rites of Passage for Boys.[140] The Cultural Awareness Series, that continues to be an annual highlight, was begun in 1994. It highlights the contributions of African Americans in the development of the country and its history.

Brooks' members come from every segment of the African Diaspora. On the website, www.brooksmemorial.org, Brooks highlights the diversity of its 25 ministries, and celebrates and invites lay leadership.

During the decade, beginning in 1994, Brooks began its life as a CRC and hosted churches from around the nation "to share with them the richness and depth of the Brook's Ministries and the actions that led to specific outcomes."[141] The vision of the congregation is stated in its application to SBC21: To make plain the gospel of Jesus Christ so that it manifests itself in the lives of its members and the people in its community through spiritual, political, and economic empowerment.

Not all of the current Black congregations began their histories as Black congregations. Emory United Methodist Church in Washington, D.C., another SBC21 Resource Center, has come to its revitalized existence in the twenty-first century, having been founded as a White congregation in 1832. At that time the church was in an area outside the city, called Brighton, on Seventh Street Plank Road, now Georgia Avenue. A history of the church, written in 1961 tells the story.[142] Persons who had been meeting in homes until that time constructed a log building on land just south of the church's present location. It was named for Bishop John Emory.

In 1843 the original building was replaced by a second log building that had a small gallery, which was occupied by the Black worshippers during services. When the church split in 1844, this history notes:

> About this time, there were civic agitations abroad in the Bladensburg District and in 1853 Emory Chapel left the Methodist Episcopal Church and joined the Virginia Conference of the Methodist Episcopal Church, South. . . . The Quarterly Conference records of November 1853 state that "a vast majority of the people at Emory Chapel are sympathetic to the southern viewpoint."[143]

Still, in 1854 Elizabeth Butler, a Black woman, sold a piece of property to Emory, and a year later she sold another half acre piece to the church. The deed for this second piece included a restrictive covenant that stated that the property "was to be used for purposes of worship and a cemetery and for no other purpose."[144] It is on this half-acre that the current facility now stands. See figure 1.8. In her will Butler directed that a third piece of property be sold to Emory Chapel, just north of the current building.[145] This does not seem unusual when one learns that Blacks were listed in the earliest membership lists. The history notes that in 1856 of the seventy-two members, thirteen were Black. A page in the 165th anniversary book contains a page from the Church's register that lists names of thirteen "Colored Members 1854-1855": John Addison, Truman Butler, Eliza and Franklin Hinton, Mary and Peter Carroll, Joseph and Sarah Simms, and Mary Williams [Spellings of names seem uncertain]; one is listed as "dead" and three as "gone."[146] The remaining nine are listed as members in 1857–1858.

It is clear that Emory Chapel and its descendent congregations have had a varied past in relationship to Black members. By 1968 the pastor, Rev. Edwin H. Langrall, was the subject of an article in the *Washington Post*. In it he related a strange metaphor that came to him in his semi-delirium while recovering from mumps. It led him to define and share with his congregation his hopes for change at Emory, which would "tax the thinking of his congregation." The article quotes him as saying, in part: "The main thing is keep [the congregation] here. I think the future will eventually swing in our favor."[147]

The article goes on to say:

> His concept envisions a Negro in the pulpit. "If we had a Negro pastor," he says, "we would lose 90 percent of the whites we have already. However, I'm sure that if the church could survive with the 10 per cent, the right man would win the neighborhood.[148]

He spoke prophetically; but his vision took almost 30 years to be fully validated.

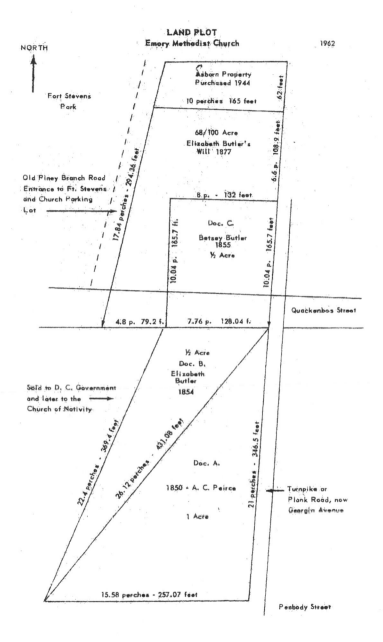

Fig. 1.8 The Land Plot of Emory United Methodist Church. 1962, F. Lee. Margaret Fisher, 1962.

Victoria Campbell Hamilton came to Emory in 1968. She remembers:

> As I walked in the church, I noticed that the congregation was white. I
> was warmly welcomed at the door by the ushers. As the ushers seated
> me, the congregation looked at me, some with smiles, some without.
> After the worship service the Pastor, Rev. Langrall gave me a warm wel-
> come and invited me to come back. Later that year I became a member.
> One Sunday the choir director walked down the isle [sic], heard me
> singing and told me that I had a strong voice and encouraged me to join.
> Norma Vinson and I were the two black members in the choir at that
> time. I became very active in the church and I noticed many members
> drifting away so Norma and I started inviting our families and friends to
> visit Emory.[149]

Vesta Schwartz recalls coming to the church in 1971:

> At the time the members were mostly white with a few blacks and they
> warmly welcomed me to the fellowship. There was a genuine feeling of
> love and affection and I decided rather quickly to join the church. The
> organist Mrs. Gertrude Parsons was quite enthused about my interest in
> the Sanctuary choir. She invited me to join and I did so without any
> reservation....
>
> In the 70s and 80s as history would have it, the flight of the majority of
> the white members to the suburbs resulted in a decline of human and fi-
> nancial resources at Emory. During that time there was a gradual increase
> in black membership...
>
> Despite all these and other adversities, the small remnant of thirty to
> forty souls acting on faith held fast with a strong determination to carry
> on....
>
> Under the present leadership of Rev. Joseph W. Daniels, Jr. Emory now
> has a membership of 275.[150]

Emory reached its maximum membership of 1,360 between 1941 and 1957
when Dr. Edgar C. Beery was pastor.[151] In 1976 the first Black pastor,
Stephen D. Abel, was appointed. Eight African Americans have pastored
at Emory, the current pastor has been appointed there for the last 15 years,
the second longest pastorate in Emory's history.[152]

Music has been from its beginning an important part of the ministry
of Emory. The 1962 history asserts that, "Emory has always maintained a

high standard of music in its organization."[153] It began in 1832 when Hamilton Caskell, an original member, led the music with a tuning fork for the next 29 years. In 1997 a list of all the music leaders from 1932 to 1978 are listed on a page copied from the congregations records,[154] and 6 distinct singing groups are pictured in the Commemorative Edition for the 165 anniversary.

Emory has occupied a total of two buildings on the original site, the second of which included a school, and three structures on its current site to the north: The Red Brick Church 1856–1861, The Stone Chapel 1867–1922, and The New Emory 1922–Present. During the years from 1861 to 1867 the congregation worshipped in homes.

This was made necessary by its location at the site of Fort Stevens, a fortification built during the Civil War to protect Washington, D.C. The log church was commandeered for troops, the basement was used to incarcerate unruly soldiers, and barracks and officers quarters were built on church land using timber from the trees and homes that were torn down by the soldiers: After the war, the barracks were used for worship with straw on the floor and blankets draped over openings for protection from the elements. It took almost 50 years for the government to pay the rent ($412 in 1880) for the ground and the destruction of the church property ($4700 in 1907).[155]

The words at the end of the 1962 history may forespeak the voice of Emory's current congregation. Reflecting on the fact that many members were moving out of the community, the 1962 writer noted that "changing times is [sic] showing its effect in our community" and goes on to express this hope:

> While, it is true that Emory faces problems today, our faith should remain firm, knowing that God in His wisdom has a plan for His people, and for the work of Emory. We trust that you, and others, will find this short history an inspiration and an incentive to give more of your time and effort to the upbuilding of His Kingdom here.[156]

In 1992 Emory was in a community that was transitioning to one dominated by various persons from the African Diaspora and Hispanic countries in Central and South America. It was on the verge of becoming a part of a two-point charge when Joseph Daniels was appointed. Emory's current ministry and its role as CRC gives life to this hope expressed over 40 years prior.

You can learn more about Emory and other congregations by viewing the DVD included with this publication.

St. Marks, Brooks, and Emory opened themselves to being resource centers to help strengthen the ministries of Black congregations in the twenty-first century. This is a century in which the story of Black Methodists will continue, as the descendents of those Black Methodists who helped give birth and life to this uniquely American denomination continue to do so. They celebrate the election of 30 Black bishops since the union of 1968,[157] continue the faithful and vibrant discipleship that marked their beginning, and respond to the changing cultural conditions in which they do mission. They, along with the other CRCs, have shared their gifts with Black congregations and now share them with the wider Church. They are aware of the dilemma that faces the entire United Methodist Church: retaining tradition and addressing progress.

In *The Story of American Methodism*, Norwood states:

> If hundreds of thousands of black Americans are now members of Negro Methodist denominations which have broken off from the mainline parent body, the original responsibility for the break is not theirs. The validity and value of their traditions can be ignored only at the peril of future prospects for Methodism in America.[158]

But this is also true of the Blacks who stayed and of those who have come over the years to worship, serve, and be in mission and ministry as Black Methodists in The United Methodist Church. They can be found in a wide variety of congregations like Zoar, St. Mark, St. Paul, Emory, Asbury, Roberts Memorial, Brooks Memorial, and Windsor Village United Methodists Churches. It is to their work and ministry, during the years of the SBC21, to identify and now share the validity and value of their traditions and their strategies in dealing with the present that we now turn.

NOTES

1. James S. Thomas, *Methodism's Racial Dilemma: The Story of the Central Jurisdiction* (Nashville: Abingdon Press, 1992), 15.
2. Dwight Culver, *Negro Segregation in the Methodist Church* (New Haven: Yale University Press, 1953), vii.
3. United Methodist Church, "African Americans Gather to Remember Central Jurisdiction" (by Pamela Crosby), 2004, 3. http://archives.umc.org/interior.asp?ptid=2&mid=5595.

4. John Hope Franklin, *From Slavery to Freedom: A History of Negro Americans*, 5th ed. (New York: Alfred A. Knopf, 1980), 24.
5. David Briddell, "Strengthening the Black Church for the 21st Century Initiative, 2004 General Conference (2005–2008), 4.
6. Marilyn Magee Talbert, *The Past Matters: A Chronology of African Americans in The United Methodist Church* (Nashville: Discipleship Resources, 2005), 26.
7. Christian Timelines. http://www.christiantimelines.com/aa_church.htm
8. Talbert, *The Past Matters*, 30. "[In 1766] Philip Embury, Methodist minister, began preaching in his cousin's house, Barbara Heck. Attending the first meeting was Philip, Barbara, Barbara's husband, a hired hand (White), and a Black servant. This servant's name was either Betty or Bettea. This meeting plus the Strawbridge meeting (previously mentioned) were the first Methodist class meetings in America, with Blacks being present at both" (Christian Timelines).
9. Talbert, *The Past Matters*, 42.
10. Report on Strengthening the Black Church for the 21st Century," Report No. 3, (Petition Number: 21677-GJ-NonDis-OS; GCOM, 1996), 1996 General Conference (1997–2000), 582.
11. Fergus M. Bordewich, *Bound for Canaan: The Underground Railroad and the War for the Soul of America* (New York: HarperCollins, 2005), 86.
12. Ibid., 97.
13. Franklin, *From Slavery to Freedom*, 168.
14. Ibid., 169.
15. C. Eric Lincoln, and Lawrence H. Mamiya, *The Black Church in the African American Experience*. (Durham: Duke University Press, 1990), 66.
16. Vincent Harding, *There Is a River: The Black Struggle for Freedom in America* (New York: Harcourt Brace Jovanovich, 1991), 44, 45.
17. Talbert, *The Past Matters*, 63.
18. Thomas, *Methodism's Racial Dilemma*, 44, 45.
19. Bordewich, *Bound for Canaan*, 87
20. Franklin, *From Slavery to Freedom*, 111.
21. Russell E. Richey, *Early American Methodism*. (Bloomington and Indianapolis: Indiana University Press, 1991), 61.
22. Bordewich, *Bound for Canaan*, 44.
23. Ibid., 98.
24. Ibid., 140.
25. Richey, *Early American Methodism*, 60.
26. Ibid., 58.
27. Ian B. Straker, "Black and White and Gray All Over: Freeborn Garrettson and American Methodism." *Methodist History* 37.1:17–18.
28. Ibid., 26.
29. Ibid., 27.
30. Thomas, *Methodism's Racial Dilemma*, 17.
31. Report on Strengthening the Black Church, 1996 General Conference, 582.
32. Harding, *There Is a River*, 67.
33. Ibid., 67.
34. Report on Strengthening the Black Church, 1996 General Conference, 582.

35. Dumbarton United Methodist Church. Mount Zion Is Born. *Dumbarton United Methodist Church Cookbook: Seasonings of the Spirit.* http://wwww.dumbarton-umc.org/cookbook

36. Homer L. Calkin, *Castings from the Foundry Mold: A History of Foundry Church Washington, D.C. 1814–1964* (Nashville: Parthenon Press, 1968), 37.

37. Fern C. Stukenbroeker, A Watermelon for God: A History of Trinity United Methodist Church, Alexandria, Virginia, 1774–1974, 1974, 161.

38. Ibid., 160–167.

39. Ibid., 197.

40. Calkin, *Castings from the Foundry Mold*, 45, 46.

41. Ibid., 74.

42. Marvin Kline, "History of Rohrersville United Methodist Church." (unpublished church document, 1971), 3.

43. Christian Timelines.

44. Saint Paul United Methodist Church, "The History of St. Paul United Methodist Church," http://www.stpumcmd.org/history3.htm, 1.

45. Ibid.

46. Ibid.

47. Ibid.

48. General Commission on Archives and History, "Zoar United Methodist Church, Philadelphia, Pennsylvania: Heritage Landmark of The Untied Methodist Church." http://www.gcah.org/Heritage_Landmarks/Zoar.htim

49. Ibid.

50. Historical markers. http://www.explorepahistory.com. Used with permission of WITF, Inc., Harrisburg, PA.

51. Lincoln and Mamiya, *The Black Church*, 47.

52. United Methodist Church, "Center Will Document History of African-American Methodists" (by Pamela Crosby), September 1, 2004, 2, http://archives.umc.org/interior.asp?ptid=2&mid=5595.

53. Lincoln and Mamiya state that "representatives of five...churches came together at Bethel Church in 1816 to officially organize the African Methodist Episcopal Church" (page 52). This is also the year that Richard Allen was elected bishop of the denomination. Some sources cite 1815 as the formal organization date of the AME church. *The Methodist Yearbook*, 1916, refers to 1815 as the official date it was "regularly organized."

54. Oliver S. Baketel, ed., *The Methodist Yearbook*, 1916 (The Methodist Publishing House, 1916), 217.

55. Franklin, *From Slavery to Freedom*, 112. According to the AMEZ Church official website (www.a.m.e.z.org), the denomination was "chartered in 1801 and firmly established in 1820, when the leaders voted themselves out of the white Methodist Episcopal Church. The next year, church founders agreed to call the church the African Methodist Church in America. But to distinguish this New York-based group from the Philadelphia Black Methodist movement . . . the word 'Zion' was added to the title during the church's general conference in 1848."

56. Oliver S. Baketel, ed., *The Methodist Yearbook*, 1930 (The Methodist Publishing House, 1930), 260.
57. Ibid.
58. Ibid., 262.
59. Baketel, 1916, 218.
60. Ibid.
61. Baketel, 1930, 262.
62. Ibid., 261.
63. Ibid.
64. Baketel, 1916, 218.
65. Baketel, 1930, 265.
66. Ibid., 261, 262.
67. Baketel, 1916, 218.
68. Baketel, 1930, 263.
69. Thomas, *Methodism's Racial Dilemma*, 18.
70. Talbert, *The Past Matters*, 45.
71. According to Ian Straker, a church historian, there are references at particular times to "The Methodist Church" that can be misleading or confusing to someone who knows that there was the Methodist Episcopal Church up to 1844, the Methodist Episcopal Church, and the Methodist Episcopal Church, South, until 1939, followed by the Methodist Church and finally the United Methodist Church. There was never a church called the "Methodist Episcopal Church North," so we are being careful to reference it differently.
72. Lincoln and Mamiya, *The Black Church*, 66.
73. Forest Stith, and Wallace Horace, compliers, "African American Methodist Church History: Key dates" (unpublished. 2006).
74. Baketel, 1916, 218.
75. Ibid.
76. Baketel, 1930, 261.
77. Thomas, *Methodism's Racial Dilemma*, 15–16.
78. Ibid., 39, 40.
79. Ibid., 39.
80. Ibid., 43.
81. William B. McClain, *Black People in the Methodist Church* (Nashville: Abingdon, 1984), 76.
82. Thomas, *Methodism's Racial Dilemma*, 43.
83. McClain, *Black People in the Methodist Church*, 78.
84. Temple United Methodist Church, "African American Pioneers in the United Methodist Church" (by Barbara Brown), February 4, 2001. http://www.templeumc.org/archives/Black_Pioneers.html.
85. McClain, *Black People in the Methodist Church*, 80.
86. Thomas, *Methodism's Racial Dilemma*, 50.
87. McClain, *Black People in the Methodist Church*, 67.
88. Thomas, *Methodism's Racial Dilemma*, 53.
89. Ibid., 55.
90. McClain, *Black People in the Methodist Church*, 89.

91. Thomas, *Methodism's Racial Dilemma*, 108, 109.

92. Ibid., 112.

93. The Committee of Five, "Study Document on Realignment of the Central Jurisdiction to the 1964 General Conference," 1964, 2.

94. Thomas, *Methodism's Racial Dilemma*, 116, 117.

95. Ibid., 121.

96. Thomas, *Methodism's Racial Dilemma*, 122.

97. McClain, *Black People in the Methodist Church*, 91.

98. Report on Strengthening the Black Church, 1996 General Conference, 582.

99. Temple United Methodist Church.

100. United Methodist Church, "Commentary: Reunion Provides Time to Reflect on Segregated Era (by Rev. Gilbert H. Caldwell), 2004, 2. http://archives.umc.org/

101. McClain, *Black People in the Methodist Church*, 94.

102. Report on Strengthening the Black Church, 1996 General Conference, 582.

103. Temple United Methodist Church.

104. Jonathan D. Keaton, chairperson, "Strengthening The Black Church for the 21st Century Spring 2006 Progress Report" (unpublished, 2006, 1).

105. Talbert, *The Past Matters*, 129.

106. Ibid., 7.

107. General Commission on Religion and Race. Black concerns. http://www.gcorr.org/committee_files?BlackConstituency/concerns.htm.

108. Report on Strengthening the Black Church, (1997–2000), 582.

109. Ibid.

110. Thelma P. Barnes, "Through the Years," in *Our Time Under God Is Now*, ed. Woodie White (Nashville: Abingdon Press, 1993), 29.

111. James M. Lawson, "The Early Days," in *Our Time Under God Is Now*, Woodie White, ed. (Nashville: Abingdon Press, 1993), 17.

112. Barbara Ricks Thompson, "The United Methodist Church's View of the Significance of BMCR," in *Our Time Under God Is Now*, ed. Woodie White (Nashville: Abingdon Press, 1993), 76.

113. Talbert, *The Past Matters*, 120.

114. United Methodist News Service. "Songs of Zion Opened Doors for Songs of Soul and Soil" (by United Methodist News Service), 2005. http://archives.umc.org/.

115. Talbert, *The Past Matters*, 74.

116. Ibid., 98.

117. Ibid., 126.

118. Ibid., 131.

119. McClain, *Black People in the Methodist Church*, 95.

120. Report on Strengthening the Black Church (1997–2000), 583.

121. June Pembroke, "The St. Mark Story: A Brief Sketch of the St. Mark UMC Heritage" (unpublished document, 2004), 2.

122. Ibid., 3.

123. Pembroke, 6.

124. Ibid., 7.

125. Ibid., 7.
126. "Eight Decades of Brooks Memorial History and Memories" (unpublished, Brooks Memorial United Methodist Church, Jamaica, New York, 2004), 2.
127. Ibid.,1.
128. Ibid., 2.
129. Ibid., 3.
130. Ibid.
131. Ibid., 7.
132. Ibid., 4.
133. Ibid.
134. Ibid., 8.
135. Ibid., 5.
136. Ibid.
137. Ibid., 7.
138. Ibid.
139. Ibid., 8.
140. Ibid., 9.
141. Ibid., 10.
142. Margaret Fisher, "A History of Emory Methodist Church 1832–1962: One Hundred and Thirtieth Anniversary" (unpublished document,. 1962).
143. Ibid., 3.
144. Ibid., 4.
145. Ibid., 7.
146. "Rites of Passage: Ministry, Music, and Mosaics: The 165th Anniversary of Emory United Methodist Church, Washington, DC, Commemorative Edition 1997" (unpublished document, 1997, 5).
147. Kenneth Dole, "Minister Cites Unusual Image," Washington Churchmen, *Washington Post*, August 10, 1968.
148. Ibid.
149. Ibid., 8.
150. Ibid., 6.
151. Fisher, "A History of Emory," 15.
152. "Rites of Passage," 14.
153. "A History of Emory," 11.
154. "Rites of Passage," 20.
155. Fisher, "A History of Emory," 7–8.
156. Ibid., 16.
157. W. Astor Kirk, *Desegregation of the Methodist Church Polity: Reform Movements that Ended Racial Segregation* (Pittsburgh: RoseDog Books, 2005), 214.
158. Frederick A. Norwood, *The Story of American Methodism: A History of the United Methodists and Their Relations* (Nashville: Abingdon Press, 1974), 19.

CHAPTER TWO

CHRIST, OUR CENTER FOR HOPE, HEALING, AND WHOLENESS

STORIES OF CHANGE

Dorothy Watson Tatem

Every three thousand miles it is necessary to change the oil in an automobile in order that its engine can function optimally. Over an interval of three thousand miles or three months, the oil breaks down and ceases to lubricate the engine. When the lubricant deteriorates, friction occurs between the moving parts of the engine and excessive heat is generated. The increased temperature expands the various parts of the engine and this can potentially result in a locking up of the parts that have become enlarged. Whenever the oil is changed, the oil filter is changed also. The function of this piece is to filter particles from the oil that flows through the engine. Remember, the engine, has all the potential to enable the car to run well, but the oil must be changed periodically.

With regularity, a local church needs to submit itself to evaluation and change in order that it may be effective and relevant to its members and community. Many local churches have come to a realization that their congregations are on the verge of a lock down; for numerous reasons they have delayed in responding to the needs in the pew and the pavement. The urging of the Holy Spirit and the necessity of change press upon them. The power for revitalization is within but it needs attention via prayer, creativity, self-examination and the anointing of the Holy Spirit. The power is already within; it needs to be accessed. Paralyzing familiarity with outdated structures may have caused deterioration of effectiveness. Before its life core is destroyed, the congregation seeks out the laity/clergy leadership training found in the SBC21 events. New oil through insights, practical suggestions, attention to questions and responses, inspiration and fervent prayer begin to lubricate the potency for change that always was within. It was merely dormant and needed a catalyst to awaken the internal power.

The amount of oil needed for a vehicular oil change varies depending on the make and/or model of the vehicle—this could be any amount between three to fourteen quarts. But the need for the oil remains the same and the oil functions in the same manner whatever the vehicle. The amount of effort towards revitalization varies among the local churches; however, self-examination, the desire to be relevant to the pew and to the pavement, and the engagement in the spiritual disciplines (prayer, Bible study, worship, and so forth) are constants. In the midst of any SBC21 training, there is the significant understanding that the present teaching moment is but a beginning of a congregational lifestyle that will cause the body to function effectively throughout its lifetime. Periodic regeneration must occur if the life of the congregation is to be vital.

This chapter presents the transformation of four congregations: St John's UMC in Texas, Grace UMC in Pennsylvania, Emory UMC in Washington, and Mt. Calvary UMC in Texas. Whether a CRC or a PC these churches have made the commitment to change in order that revitalization is a reality in the local church and in the community.

THE PRECIOUS VALUE
OF THE DISCARDED

Dorothy Watson Tatem

Used plastic cups, crumbled paper bags, discarded food, gnarled tin cans, ragged cardboard boxes, and all manner of objects littered the pavement surrounding the imposing edifice of the powder gray stone church. Its size testified that in the fifties and early sixties the church had housed a thriving congregation. One could imagine the purr of Lincolns, Cadillacs, and Oldsmobiles pulling up to the main entrance to deposit well-dressed women with expensive hats upon their equally expensive coiffures. The imagination also heard the chatter of children and their laughter was lightly punctuated by soft-voiced reprimands of mothers and fathers who cared for them. Teenagers whispered sweet secrets that only they were privy to and begrudgingly entered the sanctuary to hear anthems and classical hymns interspersed with Wesleyan songs of worship. This would have been Sunday forty or so years ago. During the course of the week, there was undoubtedly Bible study, committee meetings, choir and other rehearsals, and youth night was scheduled for each Friday.

But in 1996, debris covered the grounds and steps of the main entrance and very few persons were within the walls of the church, St. John's Downtown UMC in Houston, Texas. If one observed carefully the litter that was strewed about, one noticed that sometimes there was a life beneath. There was a turning, a stretching, and a sitting up and standing. If one looked, really looked, there were persons in various postures about the pavement, leaning against light poles, and huddled in doorways that permitted no access. A few people walked by. Automobiles sped pass. Sadly, many who saw these persons did not separate them from the discarded items all about them. The supposed glory of former decades had evaporated; dire poverty and neglect shrouded the street and the church. But in 1996, in Houston, there were 490,500 persons in church on a Sunday morning; and over 3 million doing something else. Many of the leaders who were reaching the 490,500 were proud of their numbers of attendees, but few were asking the whereabouts of those who were not connecting with the Christ. Few were asking about those lying, sitting, or standing in the litter on the pavement in the front of the church in downtown Houston.

The bishop of the Houston Area had a vision of hope and opted not to close St. John's but to invite the Rev. KirbyJon Caldwell, senior pastor of the dynamic Windsor Village, the largest United Methodist Church in the United States, to see what he could do to revitalize St. John's Downtown. The pastor accepted the challenge and in a most innovative manner assigned a couple of local pastors as shepherds of the church. The two were indeed a couple—husband and wife, Rudy and Juanita Rasmus. A group of seed persons from Windsor Village ventured forth with the two pastors. They came into the debris of lives and by the movement of the Holy Spirit prepared to resuscitate St. John's. The pastors saw themselves as managers of the sheep not the owners. Seven days a week, fourteen to eighteen hours a day, they and the team labored. They fed folk. Clothes were found to clothe people. Proposals were written for grants in order to hire staff, set up programs, and provide housing for those who had no where to go. Drug rehabilitation programs commenced and health care became an option for the invisible people too. St. John's mantra became, "We love you and there is nothing you can do about it." Repeatedly, the pastors said it, and then the lay people who ministered said it and finally, the people to whom ministry was given became givers and said to others, "I love you." Core to the life of this congregation was love for one another. "By this everyone will know that you are my disciples, if you have love for one another" (John 13:35). Jesus said this and St. John's embodied the statement. Five years of intensive ministry continued.

The sanctuary was renovated so that the chancel became a stage, and theatrical lighting illuminated the area. The chandelier was removed and replaced by recess lighting. Traditionalists kept the Internet ablaze with emails to Pastor Rudy. Many said, "Felt like I was going back to the club." The pastor listened but stayed the course. After ninety days, new people came in. These persons did not come to give or to work; they wanted the experience of worship. These were young people. After a while the new people outnumbered those who were disgruntled because their comfort zone in the sanctuary had been violated.

So many came on a Sunday morning expecting to be handed a bulletin instead they received an experience of worship. Pastor Rudy notes that one cannot predict an experience; he further acknowledges that those who look for an order of service want to control. To the unchurched, the experience was and is the cultural norm and Rev. Rudy and Rev. Juanita Rasmus agree that the pastors are 'guardians' of the cultural norm. As expected, those without the light of love left to worship and minister elsewhere. Church revenues dropped by ten percent.

To date, nine thousand persons have membership at St. John's. Five hundred give 90 percent of the $2.4 million budget. Six thousand give less than $500 annually. Another 2,500 contribute less than $50 per year. Three thousand persons of the total membership of 9,000 have no address; they were homeless or marginally so when they joined St. John's Downtown. Each Sunday, at least 200 homeless persons are intentionally invited to attend worship. Pastor Rudy calls this a "forced diversity program." Throughout the yearlong renovation, the church had moved off campus and was feeding an average of 300 persons daily in partnership with Houston Food, but these same persons were not showing up for worship. So coupons were distributed that could be redeemed after worship for something that the homeless needed. The word spread and the homeless came, redeemed the coupons and became intimate with the Christ in the process. When the church opened under the shepherding of Pastors Rudy and Juanita Rasmus, the homeless stopped attending after seven or eight months because they did not believe that they would be welcome among the middle class individuals who were filling the pews. The 'forced diversity plan' welcomed back the poor.

It was another Sunday morning and a young man in his twenties or early thirties who always carried a backpack was again at church. He had the habit of sharing a CD with people during the course of worship or soon thereafter. One Sunday after the experience of worship, he turned to a well-dressed woman beside him and gave her a CD. Haughtily, she rebuffed him because she thought the CD was stolen; she did not know nor take the time to know that the young man gave the legally acquired music to people to enjoy. It was after another worship experience that a shabbily dressed woman came gently behind a splendidly attired woman and began to massage her tense knotted shoulders. At first the latter was a bit disconcerted, because the blessing of peace had not come in a package that she would have ordered. At St. John's worship was and is an expression in words, song, dance, gifts, caring and indeed it is never predictable. People care for people and express this in their intentional behavior towards others. Worship continues to be a most blessed event that allows the Holy Spirit to be made evident in the most unexpected times and places.

More than worship went on in the sanctuary. At one feeding of the multitude, the only space that was large enough to accommodate all the people was the sanctuary. Pastor Rudy notes that those they were serving were already on the outside, and to have a part of the church as off limits reinforced their sense that society perceived them as so much clutter and debris. The homeless know when a church cares or is just checking off something on its "do good" list. One day during the feeding, the rain came in torrents and the cold made it savagely penetrate clothing and shoes. Into the sanctuary, the homeless were invited. Yes, at the conclusion of the meal, there were grits, syrup, and coffee stains tattooed on the carpet. Yes, the barriers between the homeless and those with homes were torn down. The curtain that had hindered the homeless from coming to the sanctuary for worship was torn apart. Those formerly rejected came on

Sunday because they had eaten in the sanctuary on Saturday. Pastor Rudy, Pastor Juanita and church leadership all believe that the homeless are entitled to be in a safe place to sleep, rest, eat, stand up, clap, and sing.

St. John's has always been a CRC in SBC21. As a teaching church, it has continuously evaluated its own process; a plateau has never been achieved. There is always something else to strive towards, and those immersed in poverty are perhaps its best evaluators. St. John's understands that the churches that they teach will do ministry in a different manner. This further serves as a challenge to the how and why St. John's does its ministry. St. John's proffers not extreme makeovers but ministry about people who are living at the extremes of society (even the well to do). This church teaches other congregations that becoming a caring community requires accountability to those served and those with whom one serves.

The cost of doing ministry 24/7 without regard to oneself or heeding the wise cautions of others has at separate times sent each of these committed pastors into a shattering personal crisis. In the throes of the horrific crisis, each had to find his/her way back to the self of God's creation, and review the scripting of her/his life. Each came through the ordeals over time. Each found that self-care was as vital as ministry to others. Each discovered again that the impossible possibilities with God apply to the self as well as to others. Self-reflection may possibly begin with, "Maybe . . ." Prayer and the spiritual disciplines had always been a part of their lives, but now each had caught a sobering glimpse of human limitation and the divine power that is made perfect at the juncture of inadequacy. Pastor Juanita discovered a giftedness in being a spiritual guide to individuals or to large gatherings. Her facilitations help others to avoid the abyss of the loss of self. Pastor Rudy wrote an autobiography, *Touch: The Power of Touch in Transforming Lives*.[1] In the writing, he found his own healing. Their personal sufferings have enabled each to discern and understand in a more profound manner the turbulence deep within many of the people they are divinely called to serve.

Panic was thick in the air as people fled the city by whatever means possible. A storm called Rita was coming, and she promised to be a force with which to reckon. Big churches, small churches, agencies, shelters—all were closed against nature's ensuing force. In his recent book, *Touch*, Pastor Rudy writes, "After a long time in anguished prayer, I decided that Juanita and I would stay here [Houston]. On the morning the hurricane sped like a freight train toward the city, I went downtown to the church. The streets of Houston were deserted, but the homeless people had nowhere to go.

When I walked to the door of the church, two men came up behind me. I turned around, and one of them looked at me and said solemnly, "Pastor Rudy, we knew you wouldn't leave us."[2] What really mattered in life and death seemed to be that which you could put in your car. But in the final analysis, that which mattered was human presence and its reminder of God's infinite care and precious value of those who have been discarded.

GRACE IS MADE SUFFICIENT

Dorothy Watson Tatem

The drums were stacked in a corner in the pastor's study. No stands supported them; they were just piled upon one another. From a nearby window, the sunlight and shadow played in silence on the stretched skins. A few years prior, the previous minister had given the drums to Grace United Methodist Church in Philadelphia, Pennsylvania. After four or so years, no one even noticed the drums. They had become fixtures in the pastor's study. The instruments invited no one's attention and did not confront the senses. The percussions were just there in the corner—a gift forgotten.

The church was erected in the late fifties or early sixties. Multi-hued stained glass windows color the sanctuary on sunlit days. The chancel is long with the altar on the distant back wall. Choir lofts are on either side of the area. At the front are the pulpit and the lectern. It is a building of many rooms, a glass enclosed narthex, and is situated in a middle-class African American neighborhood. Worship was traditional and quiet. Hymns and anthems comprised the music genres. The pastor preached sermons of appropriate length and there were few, if any, "Amens" heard. It was not a stiff congregation; its worship was simply predictable. Every Sunday was the same with a bit longer service on the first Sunday due to Communion.

The pastor, Dr. William Gary George, convened a SBC21 team, and this PC traveled to its first training at the Ben Hill United Methodist Church in Atlanta, Georgia. For the team, the Sunday morning worship experience was the most stunning event of that training weekend. During the service, the large choir of over sixty persons sang gospel music and hymns. They sang in full volume, joyous rhythm, and with a swing and sway. Soloists "got ugly" when they gave praise in song. The choir sang with the whole of its physical as well as spiritual being. It seemed as though a musical offering was being given unto God. Accompanying the choir was a baby grand piano, a keyboard, drums, and an organ. The keyboard could make the sounds of strings and any other instrument deemed necessary, while the pianist skillfully offered up chords that rounded out the sound. It was delicious music.

At Grace United Methodist in Philadelphia the drums in the pastor's office were silent and untouched. They were not the order of the day in worship. A quiet, prescribed, dignified worship proceeded with a guest preacher who was substituting for Dr. George who was in Atlanta with the five members of Grace's SBC21 team.

At Ben Hill, the sermon was delivered as though the pastor would never, ever have the opportunity to preach again. He preached as though this was his one chance to challenge, teach, and invite the congregants to become part of the Kingdom of God, gain strength, encouragement and hope for the situations in their lives. Application of scripture was clear, and all knew that they were to go out, tell how God had moved in their lives, and invite others to become disciples of Jesus Christ. In the excitement of the proclamation, folk were talking back to the preacher! In the filled-to-capacity sanctuary, one could hear loud, "Amens," "Say so," "Preach" from all corners. Sometimes, it seemed as though the pews were on fire when individuals leaped up to call forth their responses to a portion of the sermon which resonated to something in their lives. These were middle class and educated African American persons enthusiastically involved in a holy encounter.

The team from Grace watched amazed at the demonstration of such fervor and focus in worship. Yet, on second thought, the behaviors were not really strange to them for many as children had parents, grandparents, guardians or some relatives who were expressive in worship. Now as adults, they had chosen to worship with more dignity. But here in Atlanta, five members of Grace in Philadelphia, Pennsylvania were experiencing worship as a Pentecost moment that was obviously the norm not the exception to Sunday mornings at Ben Hill United Methodist Church. (And some of them would find the same dynamic at Teresa Hoover in Arkansas, St. John's Downtown in Houston and St. Luke Community in Dallas—all United Methodist Congregations.)

At the conclusion of the sermon came the altar call.[3] People poured out of the pews to get to the altar rail. The music and the sermon had moved their hearts to seek and trust in Jesus Christ. People joined Ben Hill for continuing nurture, and individuals came forth in need of prayer for the vicissitudes of their lives. Some of the members of Grace had lugged personal difficulties all the way from Philadelphia to Atlanta. They too found their way to the altar. Some remained seated including one woman who had sensed a call to do a particular ministry at Grace but had procrastinated because under the former pastorate she had received no support. She was reluctant to approach the present minister. The weight of the call to do ministry was greatly upon her, but she sat determinedly in her pew at Ben Hill that Sunday morning.

In Philadelphia, the doors of the church were reverently opened inviting whosoever to join. No one came. A call for those in need of prayer was given. A few came forth to kneel at the rail of the altar.

Simultaneously, in Atlanta, the woman sat quietly in her pew seeming to be quite calm and poised though the call to initiate ministry weighed heavily upon her. After a few minutes a young female associate pastor came to her pew and prayerfully laid hands on the woman's shoulders. The minister then admonished her to return home and do that which the Lord was impressing upon her to do. The woman from Grace was astounded, but also certain that she had just received an affirmation and confirmation from her Lord. Other members of the Grace team discovered that they had somehow been relieved of the burdensome quality of their circumstances. Their situations at home had not been amended, but they had experienced hope and newfound faith that God would be with them and intervene in their problems.

In Philadelphia, persons quietly left the church with some glimmer of hope for their lives and with dignity they went their several ways.

At the conclusion of the service in Atlanta, the SBC21 team from Philadelphia was jubilant about its encounter with the Lord that morning. They had sung, swayed, clapped, talked to the preacher, and prayed with a heightened sense of the Savior's presence. This spiritual feast could not be quarantined at Ben Hill. No, No! The team was already visualizing ways of adapting all that they had learned in the worship seminar and had experienced in worship. The knowledge learned and the experience were going to be transported and adapted in Philadelphia. They wanted to experience God's power in the environment of Grace. They knew that if they were willing, God would use them to move in abundant grace among the people at Grace.

Then it happened. Someone remembered the drums in the corner near the window in the pastor's study. The person inquired of Dr. George about setting them up in the sanctuary. His response was affirmative. The worship experience at Ben Hill in Atlanta had given Grace in Philadelphia permission to have drums and all manner of instruments in the sanctuary. Home they flew to the city of Brotherly love (and "Sisterly Affection"). Stands were purchased for the drums. Gleaming chrome now supported the percussion instruments, and they were set up in the sanctuary a short distance from the organ. They looked so impressive and professional. Grace had made a first step, and they did so being fully aware that there was no percussionist to give voices to the drums. But hope had been born anew and faith had been quickened in the spirits of the team by the training and worship at Ben Hill on that faithful weekend. They came home and one-on-one or to groups they testified about what they had heard, learned, and seen. Anyone who would listen heard of the marvelous training and of the vibrant life-giving, spirit-awakening worship. The people of Grace heard of the impossible being made possible and faith being the essence of that which was hoped for and the evidence of that which was not yet seen (Hebrews 11:1).

So the drums now set in the sanctuary being brushed only by the blue hue cast by the large stained glass window opposite them. Then came the day that one of the college students at Grace returned home. He gave voice to the drums! A new rhythm was added to worship. People stood and moved in their pews as they had not done before. The preaching moment fervently challenged, admonished, and invited to discipleship. Hope, faith and love became almost palatable during worship.

A trumpeter was later hired.

Then a guitarist was contracted.

The pastor kept right on preaching with the excitement that came from his immersion in scripture, prayer and study. Sometimes, he even ventured out of the pulpit during the course of the sermon.

A saxophonist was hired.

People found release from the strangleholds of the difficulties in their lives. They were taught how to apply scripture to every aspect of their lives.

A mass choir came into being and gospel music filled the air with joy and victory.

A male choir was formed. Proclamation to the glory and power of God rang forth in song through base and tenor voices. The very existence of this group said to the men who entered the church that God's divine grace was sufficient for brothers also.

Pastor George extended invitations to salvation. People gave themselves to Christ. When the doors of the church were opened for membership, the people joined Grace United Methodist Church in Philadelphia.

The woman of the Grace SBC21 team who had received prayer and instruction to following God's leadings at Ben Hill, returned to Philadelphia and began a ministry for children.

There was an interval when the pastor attempted to wear causal clothes instead of a suit or robe on Sunday morning. When he preached in the new attire, lips pursed and faces were expressionless with silent disapproval. Emails confirmed what the pastor had observed. Seeking to be flexible but always moving the church towards greater ministry in worship and beyond the walls of the building, he acquiesced and returned to traditional attire on Sunday morning.

The youth became a voice in the life of the church and regular liturgists on Sunday morning. Hospitality abounded. To enter the doors of the sanctuary was to be greeted by an usher of any age, and on special occasions, there were striking church-name imprinted tee shirts that instantly identified those who greeted guests and might be of assistance to the stranger in the midst of the congregation.

Dr. George notes that Grace is yet a traditional church. On the first and second Sundays, anthems and hymns are the musical forms sung with new vitality. Many anticipate with great expectation the third and fourth Sundays for these are the days of the new choirs, the instruments, and the beauty of liturgical dance. The preaching is always fervent. In the final analysis, Grace United Methodist holds forth to all seeking intimacy with God, options that keep all enveloped in the sufficiency of divine grace.

In 2007, Dr. George was appointed as district superintendent. The church transitions with a most gifted and nurturing interim pastor, the Rev. Herbert E. Palmer, and there is in the atmosphere a sense that the transformation and vitality within and without the church walls will continue. There is grace sufficient at Grace!

THE DIVINE COMMISSION

Cheryl A. Stevenson

The word of God came to Rev. Joseph Daniels as it did to Moses in Exodus 3:7-12. The "I Am" sent Rev. Daniels to Georgia Avenue in the Brightwood Community of Washington D.C. God sent this prophet to the people of Emory United Methodist Church. Hear these words of the Lord:

Then the Lord said, "I have observed the misery of my people who are in the *Brightwood Community*; I have heard their cry on account of their taskmasters (*drug dealers, slaves to prostitution* . . .). Indeed, I know their sufferings, and I have come down to deliver them from the *blight of the Brightwood Community*, and to bring them up out of that land to a good and broad land, a land flowing with milk and honey. The cry of the *Brightwoodlites* has now come to me; I have also seen how the *Brightwood Community* oppressed them. So come *Joseph*, I will send you to *Washington, D.C.* to bring my people, the *Brightwoodlites*, out of *suffocation* and *death*. But *Joseph* said to God, "Who am I that I should go to *Washington, D.C.*, and bring the *Brightwoodlites* out of the depth of *suffocation* and *death?* He said, "I will be with you; and this shall be the sign for you that it is I who sent you; when you have brought the people out of *suffocation* and *death*, you shall worship God on this mountain, *Hilltop of Emory United Methodist Church*. (Text in italics is writer's paraphrase.)

The Cry of the Brightwoodlites

Located on the hilltop of Fort Stevens, Emory's beacon of light shines throughout the Brightwood Community. The church motto is "If you don't shine, the world stays blind." The light of this congregation shines forth through the mission, which is to draw people to Jesus, disciple people to wholeness, prepare people to meet needs, and send people to develop a community of opportunity for all.

Emory can testify as to how God can revive and revitalize a church on the brink of closure. The church had been through many changes in both demographics of the community and those who occupy the pews. As discussed in chapter 1, Emory originally was a predominately white congregation that was home to many of Washington, D.C.'s powerbrokers at the turn of the century. As time progressed and the neighborhood changed the congregation began to diversify. Due to fluctuating membership and transitions in the conference and community, Emory experienced a decline that was marked by no fulltime pastoral leadership, and the Baltimore Conference on several occasions discussed closing the church. In 1992 the church was being considered to become a two-point charge, and it was at this time that the Lord sent his divine commission to Rev. Joseph Daniels through the District Superintendent. According to Rev. Daniels, Emory was on life support. The community could not feel the heartbeat of God! The church and community were suffocating; there was no oxygen, and there was no breath of life. This congregation and community needed resuscitation by God's Breath of Life!

Rev. Daniels' heart wept for the people of Emory and the Brightwood Community. The grass on the church grounds had not been cut for six years. The land was covered with alcohol bottles, beer cans, used needles from drug addictions and used condoms from prostitutes. The Brightwood Community had a reputation for drug and alcohol abuse, Georgia Avenue was known as prostitute alley, and transients hung out in the neighborhood. The cry of the Brightwoodlites brought tears to Rev. Daniels' eyes. The Lord spoke to Rev. Daniels' heart and through the tears, Rev. Daniels began to see a sign of hope and a miraculous healing for this community. The vision from God was clear. Emory was called to work with the community to overcome drug addictions, prostitution, and to give the homeless and community hope—Christ is our Center for Hope, Healing, and Wholeness!

The Spiritual Journey to the Land of Milk and Honey

Rev. Daniels believes as the pastor of Emory, he has the unique prophetic voice to address situations in the congregation and community. As pastor, he must be devoted to the development of the Brightwood Community. He must lead this community to the land of milk and honey. Therefore, the two roles of the Black Church must be to facilitate resistance to injustice and to be an organizing force in its community for liberation and freedom endeavors.

According to Rev. Daniels, when a pastor is clear about his or her call and is practicing spiritual discipline, then that positions the pastor to be a prophetic leader. The book of Nehemiah is an example. When Nehemiah became clear about his calling and practiced spiritual discipline, he was able to rise up in his prophetic gift. God could use him in a very profound way! God uses the pastor to position other people to influence others. A congregation is reflective of its leadership. There is a familiar saying: So as the pastor goes, so goes the congregation.

Upon Rev. Daniels' arrival at Emory, members only attended Sunday morning worship and Sunday school. There was no weekly Bible study or community involvement. So to position Emory to be a prophetic voice in the Brightwood Community, the congregation had to start from ground zero. Emory was spiritually dead. Rev. Daniels' first focus was on the church's spiritual development, specifically worship and discipleship. Making changes over time in worship, weekly Bible study, and particularly with

Disciple Bible Study turned the church around. These changes helped people to see not only who they were in Christ but also what their ministry responsibilities as Christians were. Through Christian identity the members began to hear the call and to launch various aspects of leadership and community development work.

The vision given to Rev. Daniels was being fulfilled through the people of Emory United Methodist Church. The first ministry was with the homeless. A few members in Disciple Bible Study sensed a call to minister to the homeless. This small group began housing homeless people in the church. They housed twelve people over a two-month period in conjunction with Capital Hill Community Services. This new partnership with a community organization provided services on how to do intake of the homeless. Reaching street people lead to the formation of a 501(C)3 corporation and the church began to do ministry under the Beacon of Light, Inc. umbrella. Today one of Emory's greatest challenges is working with the homeless to overcome addictions. The church is also beginning work with crime prevention ministry and drug abuse preventive ministry.

The pastor can be the "catalyst" for laypersons to accept their call (spiritual gifts). To reiterate Nehemiah's example, when the pastor is practicing the spiritual disciplines, God uses the pastor to position other people to influence others. The walls of the Brightwood Community were broken down. The people of Emory had to be clear about their calling. Lead by Rev. Daniels, the prayer of Nehemiah 1:5-11 filled the sanctuary walls of Emory. Revival, restoration, and revitalization of the Brightwood Community would only come through prayer and fasting.

Emory holds two major fasts per year, a Lenten Fast in the spring and a Harvest Fast in the fall (three weeks before Thanksgiving). Fasting and prayer go together; if you fast without prayer, you are starving yourself to death. Fasting and prayer is so woven into the fabric of Emory that if needed the church will hold a fast during other times to experience a breakthrough to an issue the community is facing.

Prayer Marathons are another spiritual discipline Emory practices. In January 2006 Emory held a twelve-hour prayer marathon. Following were a twenty-four hour (April), a thirty-six hour (September), and a forty-eight hour (December) marathon. The members gathered with specific prayer topics, a prayer theme, and over the assigned time different people lead prayer in the sanctuary. There were ongoing periods of intercessory prayer with a specific focus such as world peace, deliverance of people in the congregation from addictions, family unit, job openings, and so forth.

You Shall Worship God on This Mountain!

He said, "I will be with you; and this shall be the sign for you that it is I who sent you; when you have brought the people out of suffocation and death, you shall worship God on the Hilltop of Emory United Methodist Church.

God is doing a miraculous healing in the Brightwood Community. The Great Commission is being fulfilled. Emory is going "therefore and [making] disciples of all nations, baptizing them in the name of the Father and of the Son and of the Holy Spirit" (Matthew 28:19). The congregation is made up of fourteen nationalities including the United States: Gambia, Ghana, Liberia, Nigeria, Sierra Leone, Zimbabwe, Guyana, Jamaica, Federation of St. Kitts and Nevis, St. Vincent and the Grenadines, Trinidad and Tobago, Haiti, and Uganda. God has resurrected Emory United Methodist Church! Now the congregation is an influential church in Washington, D.C. and the Baltimore-Washington Conference. This congregation has grown from near closure to a membership of 450. Emory has welcomed congregants who come from over 26 different countries in the African diaspora reflected by the surrounding community that it finds itself. The triumphant resurrecting history of the church has made them a congregation that believes God's promises and testifies that God can redeem and restore anything and anyone. The people of Brightwood are telling it on the mountain, over the hills, and everywhere. Following are a few of the triumphant stories.

Exhilaration of Triumph #1: Emory's lay leader has triumphed over alcoholism and philandering. After nine years in this lifestyle, this leader had a life-changing encounter with Jesus Christ that drastically changed his life. His transformation astonished the people at Emory who asked, " Isn't this the man who was an alcoholic and womanizer? Look at him now, a changed man filled with the power of the Holy Spirit." His change was similar to Paul, who was touched by a Damascus road experience. A year after his life transformation, he became a rock-solid lay leader in the church.

Exhilaration of Triumph #2: The boulders of Fort Stevens located on Emory's property is a gathering place for the homeless, and it is at this place that two homeless men have triumphed over forgiveness—a forgiveness of almost killing each other over the dispute of seven dollars. The men joined by this spirit of forgiveness now minister and serve meals to other homeless persons through Emory's New Life Ministry, a ministry that changed their language and behavior. A ministry that began on the boulders of Emory has now moved to Emory's sanctuary. A ministry where worship and prayer in a nontraditional service is transforming lives in the Brightwood Community.

Rev. Daniels, the Brightwood Community, and the members of Emory are worshipping God on the mountaintop! People are seeing their lives change for the better. People who were down and out are getting back up again. The brokenhearted have a new sense of hope. Families are coming back together again. There is a spiritual revival in the new land of Brightwood Community!

Emory transitioned from being a PC to being selected as a CRC in 2002. Inspired and empowered by SBC21 training events, Pastor Daniels and the leadership are now sharing their transitional story with PCs. Their story of hope, healing, and wholeness enables them to nurture, empower, and train other churches for mission and ministry. This is the beauty of SBC21. One church sharing challenges, triumphs, experiences, and learning tools with others to strengthen the whole church.

TEACH THEM HOW TO FISH IN THE WATERFALLS OF LIFE

Cheryl A. Stevenson

Mt. Calvary United Methodist Church, located in Wichita Falls, Texas, is teaching the community how to fish in the waterfalls of life. Rivers of life transformation are flowing through the streets of Wichita Falls. The sound of rushing waters and the thunderous voice of God in Amos 5:24 is flowing through the community: "Let justice roll down like waters and righteousness like an ever-flowing stream." Mt. Calvary is responding to the voice of God that demands justice and righteousness.

The church is located on the Eastside in a low-income community with a high unemployment rate. Many vacant houses are visible and many homeless walk the streets to try to find a place of refuge in the neighborhood. Appointed to Mt. Calvary in October of 1997, Rev. Sylvester Shed is leading this small congregation (less than 100 members) as they fulfill the divine calling of God to feed the homeless, heal the sick, preach the word, and make disciples of Jesus Christ. On the first Sunday Pastor Shed preached twelve people were in attendance. This is a significant number and a sign from God because Jesus had twelve disciples. The Lord sent twelve disciples on that Sunday morning to hear and respond to God's word. Rev. Shed had a meeting with the twelve to discuss the vision and future of Mt. Calvary.

In his quest to fulfill the vision the Lord had given him, Rev. Shed attended an Institute on Church Growth and Evangelism in 1998 at Saint Mark, a CRC in Wichita. This SBC21 training held at Saint Mark, under the pastoral leadership of Rev. Tyrone Gordon, inspired Rev. Shed to move forward with the evangelistic vision of ministering to the homeless. Following this encounter Rev. Shed and a team from his church then attended SBC21 training at St. John's UMC in Houston in 1999 and 2001. St. John's model of ministering to the homeless was a good match for Mt. Calvary. The hearts of the Mt. Calvary team were strangely warmed as they begin to vision together on how they would fulfill God's vision of ministering to the homeless and unemployed in their community. Thus, Power Meal, a feeding ministry for the homeless was born. Initially this ministry met resistance from the church board because of a lack of funding. Through prayer, persistence, and funding creativity from the team that attended the SBC21 training, this weekly ministry moved forward and has blessed many men and women. Yet, this ministry not only gives the homeless something to eat, but also teaches them how to fish.

Teaching the Homeless to Fish —Scene One

Like the rising of the sun that shatters gray skies, God, the Redeemer, removes the sin that beclouds the Eastside Community. There is hope for the hopeless. The words of God through Isaiah 44:21-22 is bringing life to this community: "Remember these things, O Jacob, and Israel, for you are my servant; I formed you, you are my servant; O Israel, you will not be forgotten by me. I have swept away your transgressions like a cloud, and your sins like mist; return to me, for I have redeemed you."

God had not forgotten about William Pace, a homeless person in the community of Mt. Calvary. William Pace was a drifter, living a life on the railroad tracks. A drifter boasting about his journeys to every state—except Hawaii—by train. A drifter who could look at the number on a train and tell you where it was headed. A drifter who had a $300 a day habit, a con artist. He was just surviving in the streets of the Eastside Community when Rev. Shed picked him up from walking, shared what Mt. Calvary was doing, and invited Mr. Pace to come to the Power Meal on Wednesday evening. This encounter with Rev. Shed changed Mr. Pace's life forever. Over time, Mr. Pace accepted Jesus Christ as his Lord and Savior. He is now a faithful servant! Through the ministry of Mt. Calvary, Mr. Pace grew spiritually and now is a certified lay speaker. Mr. Pace testifies that Mt. Calvary has made a huge impact on his life. He no longer thinks in terms of conning people but concentrates on *God Doing a New Thing* in his life!

Mr. Pace along with another homeless person transformed by Power Meal ministry initiated a Saturday evening alternative worship service. The service is nontraditional and is designed around telling stories of lives transformed through the ministry. The pastor coordinates the worship planning and offerings are placed in a special account used to help others in need.

In the summer of 2007, Mt. Calvary worked in partnership with the city to provide work projects for fifty homeless persons along with housing at night. The church is also working on providing a place for the homeless to stay when the Salvation Army is not open during the day.

Teaching the Homeless
—Scene Two

It is a cold winter night. Sam, a homeless person with one leg, is living in a cardboard house in twelve-degree weather. Sam hears familiar voices and the sound of shifting cardboard boxes. Suddenly three familiar faces find this homeless person under the cardboard boxes and place him in a warm car. Sam, smelling of urine and other smells from the outside environment, finds warmth and the touch of family as he is transported and carried up the stairs of the Salvation Army. He is so thankful these three angels from Mt. Calvary saved his life from the cold winter air. These three angels give thanks to God and through tearstained eyes go home to rest before beginning another day of ministry.

Memorial services are held at Mt. Calvary for many deceased homeless persons touched by this small church. Memorial services such as one held for the death of a homeless woman trying to find heat on a cold winter night has deeply touched the members of Mt. Calvary. In the quest to find heat this homeless woman died in a port-a-potty near the church. Mt. Calvary is now committed to providing heat on cold winter nights.

The Eastside Community has been touched by Mt. Calvary's warmth, food, medicine, transportation and housing. Mt. Calvary the catalyst for other churches to get involved with the homeless, continues to reach many with their hands of mercy and their heartfelt passion to teach others to fish rather than just giving them something to eat. Through the Eastside Community of Shalom which is adjacent to the church, Mt. Calvary continues to bring hope to the homeless, provide resources to build self-esteem, tutoring, and through networking provide information on job opportunities and upcoming events such as job fairs.

Size does not matter when doing ministry. Members of Mt. Calvary are energized and inspired by the words of Jesus in Luke 12:48b: "From everyone to whom much has been given, much will be required; and from the one to whom much has been entrusted, even more will be demanded." Mt. Calvary is a church that has Christ as its Center for Hope, Healing, and Wholeness!

NOTES

1. Rudy Rasmus, *Touch: The Power of Touch in Transforming Lives* (Houston: Baxter Press and Spirit Rising Music, 2006).
2. Ibid., p. 25.
3. "A prayer where worshipers are called to come and kneel at the altar beneath the rugged cross." Jeremiah A. Wright, Jr., "Growing the African American Church Through Worship and Preaching" in *Growing the African American Church*, ed. Carlyle Fielding Stewart, III (Nashville: Abingdon Press, 2006), 71.

CHAPTER THREE

THE VITAL
CONGREGATION

Dorothy Watson Tatem

In addressing the matter of strengthening Black United Methodist churches for the twenty-first century, it is imperative to have vital congregations lead the way. The effort to define and understand what comprises a "vital" congregation, what makes it effective and how it can be widely reproduced has commanded much attention. This is especially the case in recent years when declining size and participation by local churches in the United Methodist connection have been a source of serious concern.

Nurturing the building of new vital congregations and revitalizing existing ones has occasioned numerous studies. What is a vital congregation and how can we understand what happens to cause some congregations to experience observable growth and others to stagnate or languish? It is apparent that the nature of the ministry and level of effectiveness of the leadership are critical variables in the development of vital congregations. Critical studies have been undertaken to better understand what is required. It is deemed informative to consider what has been learned from the studies and then offer a general definition of a vital congregation.

In his book *Doing the Gospel: Local Congregations in Ministry*, Bishop Roy C. Nichols provides a comprehensive exploration of congregational vitality and supports his observations and conclusions with illustrative case studies. Early on he notes:

> Congregation vitality is more than a bustling program of activities. Rather, it is doing the will of God, as set forth in the Scriptures and clearly delineated in the teaching of Jesus. Congregational vitality is descriptive of a quality ingredient that is more important than size. The pews may be packed, but if the church is programmatically a glorified country club, an emotional entertainment center, or a somber cult presided over by a spiritual guru, it does not qualify as a vital Christian congregation—regardless of its numerical or financial strength.[1]

The questions proposed in a nine-point inquiry to United Methodist bishops give some indication of basic assumptions about vitality.[2]

- Serious engagement in lay training and the utilization of laity in significant ministries.
- Effective goal setting procedures employed within the context of its missional statement of purpose and a diversified ministry aimed at serving the real needs of people.
- A balanced lay/clergy conception of ministry.
- Strong in the programmatic areas of Christian education and small personal growth groups, a responsibly intertwined mission and social action, and a level of stewardship commensurate with its potential.
- A Christ-centered, biblically-based approach to ministry.
- Effective lay/clergy evaluation procedures.
- Average attendance at Sunday school, church, small groups, etc. considerably beyond that of the typical congregation.

These assumptions are effective as dynamic congregations consistently exercise their existence in three areas: leadership, nurture/outreach, and administration. The leadership believes in the future and collaboratively and assertively fashions vision, planning, and administrative structure to bring the future into time and space. Leadership views the organization as continuously mobile; the past is a vehicle of learning that instructs present steps towards tomorrow. In other words, the past dictates present steps towards becoming.

Nurturing or care for the other is the second key component of a vital congregation. Attention to the individual as well as the corporate body through a multiplicity of options lessens the possibility that persons will leave soon after initial encounters. Twenty-first century work and leisure schedules vary vastly, therefore, people need a variety of choices in order that they may find a place in the congregation that is commiserate with their lifestyles. Leadership nurture is also critical in order to avoid stagnation in the ranks or burnout from overload of responsibilities.

The vital congregation is not turned inward but is keenly aware that its life and stability are grounded in continual involvement in outreach. The pew and the pavement, the church and the community, are in constant dialogue and partnership. The church is perceived as an integral part of the community in which it is located and the community sees itself as a team with the local church member in efforts on its behalf. Whether in worship or mission this symbiotic relationship fosters life in the community and the church.

Administration is never an afterthought or a rigid entity in the vital church. Organizational structure exists to facilitate the introduction and the sustaining of relevant ministry; structure also enables the ready dissolution of ministry that has ceased to be effective. Administration is a priority of all, rather than the sole possession of a few.

A fundamental characteristic of the vital congregation is pastoral leadership. Nichols called this trait "the key."[3] He delineates eight observations, the first being that vital pastors are indispensable to vital congregations, and they possess six important qualities.

- They try very hard to model the gospel they proclaim.
- Their motivation grows out of a well-conceived theology of ministry. Even when their theological self-description seems to be fixed, these pastors tend to be genuine Christian leaders who can relate to people with varying theological points of view. They tend not to be dogmatic. They all seem to be consciously growing spiritually, "going on to perfection."
- Most of them have done special reading or taken special training in the area of church growth and vital congregation development.
- The enthusiasm of these ministers creates an anticipatory climate in the congregation that inspires and motivates the laity.
- They have uniformly had an experience of the meaning of the grace of God in their own personal lives.
- They love people.[4]

Nichols explores other observations about a vital local church, which can be paraphrased as follows. One, the theological label of the congregation or pastor does not guarantee vitality. Vital congregations can spring up anywhere, whether the population is increasing, static or decreasing. They grow because their many-sided ministries appeal to a variety of human needs. Two, vital congregations actively pursue a threefold approach to ministry: leadership, nurture/outreach, and administration. Three, until seminaries are able to devote resources and attention to the practice of local church ministries, or until the general church develops a superior intern program, judicatories will need to provide local church pastors with select reading materials for cultivating vital local church ministries and to require seminars and workshops for skills development. Additionally judicatories will need to use pastors of vital churches to give leadership in teaching education, and provide opportunities for pastors to receive further depth in the spiritual, theological, and biblical dynamics of the vital local church. Finally, there should be emphasis on raising the level of Christian influence in the life of the congregation and the community.[5]

One pastor of a United Methodist congregation that is rapidly growing in effectiveness of ministry and size has written a book that conceptually and experientially approaches the work of church growth. He intentionally focuses on African American congregations in predominantly white protestant denominations. Carlyle Fielding Stewart, III, in his text *African American Church Growth: 12 Principles for Prophetic Ministry*, cogently presents the case for what he calls "prophetic ministry."

Building on the central thesis that the "black church can build viable congregations within mainstream denominations by employing principles of church growth that reflect a prophetic concern for the ethos and life of the African American experience," he maintains that the prophetic-relational components of church growth have not been addressed.[6] For Stewart, "prophetic ministry is the critical method for vitalizing Black congregations." He defines prophetic ministry in this way:

> The process of calling the people of God into an awareness of God's saving, liberating, and redemptive acts so as to compel the radical participation of individuals and communities in spiritual, social and personal transformation. The result of that transformation will be the realization of human wholeness and potential in the present, as well as in the future.[7]

A vision that supports the value of African American culture in worship, biblical exploration, and social outreach is critical. Positive reinforcement of black culture and biblically-based preaching and study that are inclusive of African heritage are essentials. The culture is rich in musical heritage, and thus the forms of sacred music move smoothly from classical to jazz. Preaching must speak to the spirit realm, inspire for the future, and be grounded in relevant application of the text to the concerns individually and corporately at any given interval of time. Rituals are valued demarcations in Black culture, and so they find a meaningful place in the life of the Black congregation and its community.

Throughout its history African American culture has recited brilliant and courageous black women and men who have been role models for their own and other peoples. Therefore, the prophetic Black Church nurtures the leadership of males and females in all areas of ministry in the church. The people in the community see positive reflections of themselves in the local church; they partner with the congregation in services, celebrations, and come to identify with the fellowship of Christ.

The literature reviews not only in this chapter but also in other sources lead to the inference that certain characteristics are inherent in the vital congregations. These traits may be posited as follows:

1. A vial congregation is a local church of any size, with the leadership of an informed, educated, creative, energetic, biblically, and theologically grounded pastor, who has formulated and implemented a plan of ministry. The plan includes a holistic vision and mission statement for the ministry of the church. It is implemented to meet the personal and individual as well as the group and social needs of the members and the surrounding community. The ministry is holistic or balanced, paying attention to relationship with God, the neighbor, and others in the midst of life together in community.

2. A vital congregation takes seriously the full range of developmental, spiritual, social, and material needs of persons and groups of all ages, both genders, those with specialized needs and cultivates and educates the laity for participation and leadership in God's mission though the ministry of the church. Passionate and compassionate responses that emulate the love and justice of God characterize vital congregations.

3. A vital congregation pays close attention to its gathered life in which worship, singing, devotion, prayer, praise, and preaching in the varied traditions of the African American churches and communities are pursued without apology.

4. A vital congregation emphasizes Bible study in small group contexts and the use of interpretive principles that promote understanding

and bring the biblical message to life in contemporary situations and conditions.

5. A vital congregation depends on effective planning and administration in which comprehensive and broad-based approaches to ministry are undertaken on a day-to-day basis. Evaluation is an indispensable part of ministry. This includes the prophetic ministries of worship and celebration, pastoral care and support, innovative education, evangelism, mission, stewardship, and discipleship.

6. A vital Black congregation taps into the deep streams of spirituality in the heritage and life of Black people and necessarily informs, interprets, investigates, and acts on the needs, problems, and issues arising from the social-political, cultural, and economic aspects of life in church, community, nation, and world.

Conflict is inherent in change and the local church does not escape this dynamic. Whether the congregation aims to make small changes in order to remain vital or whether major alterations are required in order that the local church may continue to exist, conflict is inevitable. All congregations whether small, medium, or mega will experience tensions in the face of change. We are all comfortable with the familiar even when we sense that stagnation is occurring. Invariably, something external to ourselves prompts us to face the necessity for change; however, our first response may be to fight tooth and nail with the instigator of change or to take flight. Perhaps, we find ourselves embracing the change, but we have an attitude of confrontation towards those who are more cautious or resistant. Others of us may be passively aggressive; we won't engage in the battles; however, we won't lend any kind of support to anything while the furor is going on. The Rev. Kirbyjon H. Caldwell, pastor of the Windsor Village United Methodist Church in Houston, Texas that has a membership of 16,000 persons, posits that where there is no change, there is no growth. The absence of growth signals the proximity of death. In his book, *The Gospel of Good Success*, he makes a profoundly critical declaration: "Change and conflict are signs of life."[8] The church partnerships facilitated by SBC21 enable conflict to be perceived as manageable and integral to growth in a local church.

African Americans have a proud heritage as United Methodists dating back to 1758. This presence has resulted in a strong and vital witness in congregations and the world; lives and communities have been transformed. The Black United Methodist church has given birth to liberation and empowerment of an oppressed group. SBC21 has acknowledged the significant number of vital, growing, and effective Black congregations many of whom inspire churches across the denomination.

As the church moves through the twenty-first century, there is the need for continued and expanded witness of the Christ in a hurting and hungry world. While there are strengths to celebrate, it is critical that there be vital Black congregations to address stagnation and demise in other local churches and communities. The contexts are rural, urban, suburban, and transitional communities. The SBC21 plan includes a holistic vision and mission statement for the ministry of the church. It accomplishes this vision by meeting the individual and corporate needs within the local church and in the community in which it is located. The SBC21 plan partners congregations seeking revitalization with vital congregations that are in a continual state of transformation in order to respond relevantly to the demands of the twenty-first century.

In the final analysis, we are not talking about building awe-inspiring cathedrals or great monuments of ministry. Jesus said that the first great commandment is that we should love the Lord our God with all our heart, and with all our soul, and with all our mind. Jesus noted that the second great commandment is very much like the first; we should love our neighbor as ourselves (Matthew 22:37-40). SBC21 trainings and partnerships admonish pastors and laity to love God and the people in the pew and on the pavement. This love is the essence of regeneration. God is love (I John 4:16b). This love does not easily give up, but such love knows and accepts the shortcomings of laity and clergy. Both must commit to working with and through difficulties in order that the Kingdom of God may be realized on the earth that is being tortured by violence, neglect, and greed.

> *I give you a new commandment, that you love one another. Just as I have loved you, you also should love one another. By this everyone will know that you are my disciples, If you have love for one another (John 13:34, 35).*

NOTES

1. Roy C. Nichols, *Doing the Gospel: Local Congregations in Ministry* (Nashville: Abingdon Press, 1990), 18.
2. Ibid., 20.
3. Ibid., 177–199.
4. Ibid., 149.

5. Ibid., (observations paraphrased) 150–51.

6. Carlyle Fielding Stewart, III, *African American Church Growth: 12 Principles of Prophetic Ministry* (Nashville: Abingdon Press, 1994), 18.

7. Ibid., 22.

8. Kirbyjon H. Caldwell, *The Gospel of Good Success: A Road Map to Spiritual, Emotional and Financial Wholeness* (New York: Simon and Schuster, 1999), 230.

CHAPTER FOUR

CHARTING THE JOURNEY

Cynthia A. Bond Hopson

Journey. Just saying the word evokes an image—one that begins in a little church in the country with an old man kneeling in the amen corner praying the same prayer every Sunday morning. "Lord, bless my church. Help me to tell men, women, boys and girls that the wages of sin is death and the gift of God is everlasting life," he fervently and faithfully prayed. Plain and simple, the church, more particularly, the Black Church, was on a mission in the world: save souls, make disciples, and be a beacon of hope and light amidst the darkness on our way from here to eternity.

That journey we undertook so many generations ago is moving us along different paths but its purpose has not changed. We still must tell men, women, boys and girls that God loves them unconditionally, no matter who they are, where they are, or where they have been. Today, more than ever before, we must be moving forward, plotting and persevering, strategizing and striving to meet the challenges of crumbling families and neighborhoods, societal ills, poor health, brokenness—our own and that of the world—to create a new model for a future that is strangely familiar but vastly different. Songwriters Andrae and Sandra Crouch's classic song "Jesus Is the Answer" remind us that while technology isolates and liberates, and frequently status and the trappings of success distract us, Jesus still is the answer for the world. We just have to be about our business in some new and creative ways.

CRCS AND PCS: A MODEL FOR MINISTRY

From everyone who has been given much, much will be demanded; and from the one who has been entrusted with much, much more will be asked." (Luke 12:48, NIV)

These words from the Gospel of Luke seem to build a powerful foundation for CRCs and PCs as they pair for effective ministry in the twenty-first century. This particular piece of the SBC21 initiative continues to bless the world and the denomination with more than 900 churches involved.

Since the demise of the old Central Jurisdiction in 1968 and the creation of the newly named United Methodist Church, African American churches have closed in record numbers according to Cheryl L. Walker, chair of BMCR and also Director of African American Ministries at the General Board of Discipleship. Since the 1968 merger formed The United Methodist Church from the Methodist Church and the Evangelical United Brethren Church, more than 500 churches have closed. Yet the world and the denomination cannot afford to have this number of dying and defunct churches continue to grow. SBC21's goals had to be how to intervene and keep the churches intact, growing and healthy, and resurrect those that were dying. Creating CRCs and PCs was a logical next step. As the problem of dead and dying churches loomed large, one of the mistakes church growth experts hoped to avoid was a "one size fits all" mentality. While one size may fit most, certainly what works in Dancyville, Tennessee may not get much attention in Dallas, Texas.

Inviting churches to resource centers to not only hear about how things work but also to see them working, transforming and renewing churches, is priceless for congregants and communities. Forming the partnerships between the Davids and Goliaths also offers an opportunity for sustained growth and ministry. According to Vance P. Ross, associate general secretary at the General Board of Discipleship the initiative is a helpful model:

The initiative as conceived—offering resource centers and partners— gives an opportunity for there to be mentored growth, congregation to congregation. A struggling but aspiring church can connect to a growing, thriving church and be tutored through phases in worship, Christian teaching, and holistic stewardship. The denomination has never had a better model for teaching church growth connectionally that I've seen or heard of. Mt. Calvary United Methodist Church in Wichita Falls, Texas and its community development ministry connected to Theressa Hoover United Methodist Church in Little Rock and both demonstrate effectiveness that's not meager but that happens in places where there are economic struggles that can effect change in the community.[1]

Dr. Robert P. Gardner was pastor at the Covenant/New Hope St. Paul Charge in the Paris District of the Memphis Conference, and he and his wife, Jackie, attended one of the SBC21's training events held at St. Mark United Methodist Church in Wichita, Kansas. There they met a literal who's who of the Black United Methodist Church—the Rev. Kirbyjon Caldwell, Rev. Tyrone Gordon, Dr. Zan Holmes of Dallas and others. The lively worship, powerful preaching, and relevant workshops inspired the Gardners. He went home and assessed his three congregations and found the New Hope church the most receptive to some of the things he had learned and wanted to try. New Hope was in a rural setting but poised for growth as the community attracted new families. Gardner commented on the training:

> It worked and it was definitely useful. The idea was of stronger churches partnering with weaker churches and producing these training events that gave us some insight on how to strengthen our churches. There wasn't a one-on-one partnership, but you had larger churches that were like a learning laboratory, that showed how things were done, things like how to evangelize, usher and greeting ministries and the information was good. St. Paul was a great laboratory—I took the book Tyrone Gordon wrote and I actually made a teaching lesson at choir rehearsal several Saturdays and the people were receptive and it really helped out. The material was good and like anything else, it will work if you work it. And again, some things will work and some things won't.[2]

Gardner said the evaluation process asked how the connections could be improved, but he does not remember having an opportunity for one-on-one mentoring or monitoring. He believes that would have been helpful, but his experience more than five years ago was deemed worthwhile and meaningful. He said most large-church pastors don't have time for follow-up input into these partner congregations because everybody is busy, but he believes that would help sustain the changes that congregations decide to make along the road to revitalization.

Sometimes revitalization adjustments are major, like moving a congregation to a more visible and convenient spot and adding facilities to accommodate the growth. Other times it may be little things like having a casual Sunday that will make a big difference. In some instances better signage, attention to details like greeting each visitor, having the members wear nametags so the visitors are not singled out, broadening the definition of worship to include different music and attire, providing opportunities for small-group Bible study, caring for the poor and the homeless, ministering to prisoners who are housed in local jails and prisons and caring for their families while they are incarcerated, a focus on evangelism, diversity, outreach, immigration issues—all of these have emerged as revitalization and ministry tools.

Most participants in the CRC-PC trainings find something that they can do to add a spark or turn up the heat when they return home. The time spent away in creative imagining and holy conferencing may be just what a stagnant church needs to move it to the place where it faces the harsh realization that change is inevitable. They can manage the change or change will come, with or without them.

HOW DO WE GO FROM INEFFECTIVE TO EFFECTIVE CHURCHES AND LEADERS?

Not everything that is faced may be changed, but nothing can be changed until it is faced.   —James Baldwin

No matter where you grew up, there were always "happenin' churches" where the preaching was fiery and the choir was always inspired to "sing until heaven got the news." The sisters shouted regularly while the deacons prayed fervently and the aisles and pews were brimming with youth and young adults. Alongside them were others that were more formal, where the preaching and singing were more staid and quiet, but they too were brimming with youth. The ones that fell between the extremes seemed to flourish as well; however, as the African American community evolved, so did the church and its worship services and styles.

In some instances what emerged was what Marvin McMickle calls "two separate congregations." In *Preaching to the Middle Class* he describes an increasingly common ministry challenge:

> One church is the membership that drives into the inner city each Sunday for worship and fellowship. The other church is the people who live in the neighborhood that surrounds the church building, who turn to the church in search of hot meals, Alcoholics Anonymous (AA) support groups, day-care services, and even temporary shelter. In many instances, the first church is composed of people in the middle class, and the second church is composed of people in the underclass.[3]

Nowadays the question becomes how do you balance and/or blend these two separate congregations into one that works or two or more that can lovingly coexist for mission and ministry? No pastor makes a conscious decision to be ineffective nor does a congregation set out to be a place that people only come out of habit or because it is Sunday. Inspired worship and preaching may not necessarily yield empowered, enlightened, and active lay people; the thought and application process are much more complex than that but their development is continuous and deliberate in every way. Whether your congregation is experiencing growth, facing a steady decline, or caught somewhere in the middle, a close examination of what is going on in your church is in order and strongly encouraged. Asking the hard questions and listening closely to the answers, even the painful ones, will be critical.

The General Board of Discipleship's (GBOD) Center for Worship Resourcing undertook this task and Dean McIntyre, director of music resources, asked the agency's staff this question: "What are the characteristics or activities of a local United Methodist congregation that is actively and successfully engaged in making disciples of Jesus Christ for the transformation of the world?"[4] He grouped the answers under these broad categories: Worship and Hospitality, Ministry of the Laity, Mission-Outreach-Evangelism, Nurture, Christian Faith and Life, Education and Training, and Small Groups. The basic tenets of this compilation, listed on the following pages, have been edited for brevity and conciseness.

WORSHIP AND HOSPITALITY

These congregations (1) help worshipers encounter the presence, love, grace, call, forgiveness, comfort, power, and peace of God; (2) welcome visitors and visitors become active members; (3) have an open door policy; see the church as a hospital for sinners, not a museum of saints; (4) worship with eyes open to needs and circumstances around the church—they keep the light of Christ out front like a beacon; (5) offer numerous points of entry into congregational life; (6) love and affirm those whose lives don't measure up to conventional standards of intelligence, beauty, success, or morality, and they encourage and affirm diversity; (7) share communion every time they meet in worship.

MINISTRY OF THE LAITY

These congregations (1) emphasize that all are called to ministry through baptism; (2) have a plan for growth and development for leaders and qualitatively measure the impact (value) of what they do in faith formation; (3) have an outward focus and equip, train, and support people to be the church in the world; (4) equip people to discover and use their spiritual gifts in ministry and engage in a truly "gifts-based" ministry where the clergy's gifts are counted equally with those of laity to provide a foundation for leadership based in gifts rather than structure; (5) delegate ministry responsibilities to visit members who are sick, hospitalized, in nursing homes, or convalescing at home.

MISSION-OUTREACH-EVANGELISM

These congregations (1) help members see that their primary place of ministry is beyond the church walls so they can reach the lost; (2) ensure that the church is involved in the community in which it resides; (3) believe that community matters and value and serve the community in practical ways; (4) usher each person into a safe place within community to grow faithfully; (5) involve people in service and outreach (works of mercy); (6) witness to their faith.

NURTURE

These congregations (1) nurture and equip people through vital worship, active small groups, and challenging outreach opportunities; (2) care for and respect one another; (3) have leaders who know the names and faces of all members.

CHRISTIAN FAITH AND LIFE

These congregations (1) provide opportunities for personal growth and spiritual formation of their members' progressive journey; (2) help people develop language for talking about God in their lives; (3) engage people "where they live" and welcome them where they are; (4) pray often (corporately and privately) and teach and encourage prayer; (5) teach, equip, and encourage formative spiritual practices and disciplines, such as prayer, devotional study, and works of piety; (6) guide new converts into a personal relationship with God that creates righteous living; (7) practice good stewardship for all ages; (8) attend to justice and advocacy issues as well as mercy and compassion; (9) gather as a community of faith and scatter as a community of hope; (10) ask questions and discern the will of God together; (11) teach and show that discipleship means more than membership; (12) preach, follow, and introduce Christ in a relevant way; (13) clearly understand the fruits of the spirit, the importance of practicing faithful disciplines, and they hold people accountable for growth in and practice of faith.

EDUCATION AND TRAINING

These congregations (1) offer appropriate and effective age-level Christian education and spiritual formation opportunities; (2) offer Bible study and Bible-based Sunday school classes; (3) teach the faith; (4) engage conversations among children, youth, and adults about faith, theology, ethics, and moral behavior.

SMALL GROUPS

These congregations (1) offer content-oriented small groups; (2) have class meetings or Covenant Discipleship groups; (3) provide small-group settings for accountable discipleship.

One thing the research continues to lift up is that effective leadership among the clergy and empowered and engaged laity are keys to vibrant and vital congregations. Oftentimes the challenge for local churches is how to keep new and existing members long enough to empower them. Closing the revolving door of people who join churches but soon drift away isn't a new problem but it is still a vexing one. Vital congregations must find a way to engage all parishioners in meaningful mission and ministry and not discourage them by inundating them with meetings and mindless tasks. Much of the solution can be found in two words: build relationships.

The research is clear—dynamic and vibrant leaders beget dynamic and vibrant congregations, but how do they both become dynamic and vibrant? Dynamic and successful leaders have several traits in common according to Dr. Johnnetta Betsch Cole, America's Sister President. Cole, a former Spelman College and Bennett College for Women president, outlined six steps to effective leadership in the October 24, 2002 edition of *Black Issues in Higher Education*. She asked, "How should leadership be defined? How does one acquire the ability to exercise it?" To answer her questions, she offered these six steps:

1. Surround yourself with colleagues who are as good or better at their responsibilities than you are at yours.
2. Delegate authority and require results.
3. Model the behavior you expect of others.
4. Believe in and inspire positive change.
5. Never take yourself too seriously.
6. Serve others, not one's self.[5]

While Dr. Cole's instructions were configured for higher education, the lessons are important for pastors of new or existing congregations hoping to invent or re-invent themselves.

First, unless you're starting a church and bringing in all new people, there are people in the church that you must learn to work with. Read Dale Carnegie's *How to Win Friends and Influence People* to get started. Then take time to know your parishioners and their strengths to see what they are best suited for and then turn them loose to do whatever that something is.

One of the gripes from former pastors and lay people is that new pastors come in and make too many changes too fast without first bonding with them. The work that has been done to date by the predecessor is maligned and torn down and the churches keep starting over trying to find their niche. Before long they are weak and dying.

Second, develop a plan so that there is a talent bank waiting to be tapped. Everyone has some talent—finding out what that is offers the challenge.

In *The Empowerment Church*, author Carlyle Stewart makes this statement: "If gifts are not nurtured, then the ministry can bear little or no fruit. A number of churches have withered on the vine because they have failed to cultivate an ethos of spiritual gifting. This means developing a climate where spiritual gifts can be *explored, discovered, claimed, nurtured,* and *shared*."[6]

Again, relationship building is at the heart of vitality and vibrancy, no matter what you choose to call it or how you define it. Easum and Bandy offer suggestions for cultivating stronger and more committed Christians:

> One cannot anticipate whether the wind that energizes the Spiritual Redwood will be strong or gentle, and one cannot predict with certainty what new directions the branches and roots of the tree might take. . . . .
> Recognize a person:
> with a clear awareness of spiritual gifts,
> who is personally called by Jesus,
> and who is motivated by a strong sense of destiny.
> Anchor them in the core vision, values, beliefs, and mission
> of the organism.
> Send them into a simultaneous cascade of ministries.
> Equip them for excellence and get out of their way."[7]

Not every member wants to be engaged in the church's ministry but some do and empowering the willing is critical. Further, noninvolvement is usually not a case of laziness but parishioners may be unaware of a need that should or could be addressed and/or they may not know that their particular gift is the solution. According to Rick Warren, "The encouraging news is . . . 40 percent of all members have expressed an interest in having a ministry but they have never been asked or they don't know how. This group is an untapped gold mine! If we can mobilize this 40 percent and add them to the current 10 percent already serving, your church could have 50 percent of its members active in a ministry."[8] The more people pitch in, the better off the church and its members are. As the adage goes, many hands make light work.

We are all called to ministry whether we are the pastor, the lay leader, or the custodian, and encouraging this mindset is a good first step. Once Christians understand that there is a calling upon their lives and there is a meaningful way to demonstrate that, moving the church and moving forward becomes the focus instead of the individual.

According to Warren teaching every parishioner biblically the why and the how of this "everyone is called to ministry" concept is essential for significant church growth. He further suggests that a ministry mission statement consists of the following four pillars:

1. "Every believer is a minister." Every Christian is created, saved, called, gifted, authorized, commanded, prepared, needed, accountable for and rewarded according to his or her ministry.
2. "Every ministry is important." Some ministries are visible while others are behind the scenes, but they are all important. All the ministries are emphasized and recognized.
3. "We are dependent on each other. No single ministry is independent of the others nor can any one ministry accomplish all the church is called to do—we must cooperate and depend on each other.
4. Ministry is the expression of parishioners' "SHAPE" (an acronym for spiritual gifts, heart, abilities, personality and experiences). Each of us was uniquely designed or shaped, by God to do certain things— each person's ministry is determined by their wonderfully complex and unique makeup and understanding of what God intended for them to do."[9]

Warner said making a call to discernment and recommitment should be an annual part of your church's stewardship discussions.

Third, understand that nobody wants to go to a church where there are three or four people and there is never enough money to pay the bills. While some of these churches do not want to grow, they do not want to die either. Dysfunctional churches must be real clear —you will not attract anyone when the choir processional of two members strikes up an a capella version of "Silent Night" as they move pitifully down the aisle. The music must be attended to before any growth or revitalization takes place. Change is inevitable; embrace it and be the cause of it.

Reiland offers five "C's" that can help leaders cultivate a team spirit— "cooperation, communication, change oriented, contribution and commitment."[10] Clear, concise and deliberate communication is a good first place to start for almost anything and shared leadership is a good model. Dictatorships, whether in churches, families, or countries, foster resentment. Once the laity are demoralized and incapacitated, it will take years for that church to regroup and rebuild, if ever. When members use the gifts that are uniquely theirs, God is glorified. Of course finding that niche ministry for members comes from being a talent scout. Many world-famous entertainers were "discovered" while they were doing what came naturally. In your congregations pray for that same kind of discovery.

Defining effective congregations is an inexact science and while you may not be able to describe one, you know it when you've seen it or had an experience in one. Just because a church has increased its membership does not necessarily mean that the parishioners have grown spiritually and are equipped to do ministry. It simply means that there are some features at church A or B that attract large numbers of people. Churches that are spirit-filled and offer biblical foundations for practical living—mark the beginning of an effective congregation; however, there is more. The preaching is prophetic and also biblically based; the music is a gift from God; and those who serve have a sense of calling on their lives and have found a means to live by faith. These churches serve as a living testament of God's grace and partnerships can be forged that make a difference. Our mandate to "tell men, women, boys and girls that the wages of sin is death and the gift of God is eternal life" becomes our only song.

CHARTING THE JOURNEY STRATEGICALLY

It is very difficult to make a little change because once you start one project, you usually need to make a total assessment and do significantly more. Ask anyone who started to replace kitchen countertops. Six months and thousand of dollars later, what began as a simple project quickly consumed every waking moment. Even the scriptures warn that only a fool begins a journey without looking at what it might take to complete it, cost-wise and otherwise. Yes, there is a thin line between stepping out on faith and acting foolishly. Only your congregation can decide which is worse—making a mistake or doing nothing. Deciding to move and/or go past your congregation's comfort zone may be powerful, painful, and downright disastrous; however, not doing anything may not be an option.

Here are some things to consider during your prayer and discernment process: (1) work to build consensus before you move forward; (2) work toward gradual change initially so the idea of change does not derail your major plans; (3) make sure everyone is clear about the goals, objectives, and action plans so they can buy and sell the plan; (4) learn the words strategic plan and mission statement—they will become not just buzzwords but your roadmap for change; (5) lead by example and with sincerity and integrity, no matter what the task; (6) know and embrace success when you see it; (7) listen and explain a lot; (8) live expectantly; and finally, (8) love and recognize the past but do not let it keep you mired to past glory. Preserve the mementoes, artifacts and things that your congregation holds dear in a sacred place.

Changing your church's basic structure may be for some parishioners like having their very hearts removed. Do not discount that. Robert Lewis and Wayne Cordeiro explain "that the idea of church culture is often ignored, in part because so little material is available about it. Yet we believe that culture is to the church what a soul is to the human body. It is an overall life force that the Holy Spirit uses to give energy, personality, and uniqueness to everything a body of believers says and does. It influences everything you do. It colors the way you choose and introduce programs. It shapes how you select and train leaders."[11] These authors remind us that culture is the most important social reality in the church and though it is invisible to the trained eye, its power is undeniable. It gives color and flavor to everything your church is and does.[12]

Warren's words poignantly sum up where our journey emphasis belongs: "If we will concentrate on building people, God will build the church."[13]

AVAILABLE RESOURCES

Assistance in moving your church and worship from good to great may be as near as your local computer or Cokesbury bookstore. Many congregations report renewed life and energy after engaging in Disciple Bible Studies and the Walk to Emmaus, both offered through the General Board of Discipleship.[14] With teaching about stewardship, tithing, Bible study and Sunday school, encourage all members to participate, but especially the lay leadership team. Offer these options at convenient times, where possible, as an integral part of spiritual formation and as an opportunity for personal growth and witness. Following are resources that may be helpful for you and your congregation.

Resources

A Call to Hope: Living as Christians in a Violent Society, Vera K. White. New York: Friendship Press, 1997.

A *Ten-Week Journey to Becoming a Vessel God Can Use*, Donna Partow. Minneapolis, MN: Bethany House Publishers, 1996.

Africana Worship Book, Valerie Bridgeman Davis, General Editor; Safiyah Fosua, Associate Editor. Discipleship Resources, 2006 (www.gbod.org).

Attitude Is Everything: 10 Life Changing Steps to Turning Attitude into Action, Keith Harrell. New York: HarperBusiness, 2003.

Community with Children and the Poor: A Guide for Congregational Study, Prepared By the Task Force for the Bishops' Initiative on Children and Poverty. Nashville, TN: Cokesbury, 2003.

Cross-Cultural Conflict: Building Relationships for Effective Ministry, Duane Elmer. Downers Grove, IL: InterVarsity Press, 1993.

Culture Shift: Transforming Your Church from the Inside Out, Robert Lewis and Wayne Cordeiro with Warren Bird. San Francisco, CA: JosseyBass, 2005.

Developing the Leaders Around You: How to Help Others Reach Their Full Potential, John C. Maxwell. Nashville, TN: Thomas Nelson Inc., 1995.

Discovering Your Spiritual Gifts: A Personal Inventory Method, Kenneth Cain Kincannon. Grand Rapids, MI: Zondervan, 1981.

Eight Critical Lifetime Decisions: Choices That Will Affect the Quality of Your Life, Ralph Palmen. Kansas City, MO: Beacon Hill Press, 2001.

GBOD 2007–2008 Resource Directory: Equipping World-Changing Disciples, General Board of Discipleship. Nashville, TN, 2006.

Growing the African American Church, Edited by Carlyle Fielding Stewart III. Nashville, TN: Abingdon Press, 2006.

Growing Spiritual Redwoods, William M. Easum and Thomas G. Bandy, Nashville, TN: Abingdon Press, 1997.

Hard Living People and Mainstream Christians, Tex Sample, Nashville, TN: Abingdon Press, 1993.

Hearing God's Call: Ways of Discernment for Laity and Clergy, Ben Campbell Johnson. Grand Rapids, MI: Wm. B. Eerdmans Publishing, 2002.

How to Reach Secular People, George G. Hunter III. Nashville, TN: Abingdon Press, 1992.

Lay Leader/Lay Member: Connecting the Visions and Plans of Your Congregation and Your Annual Conference, Sandy Zeigler and Betsey Heavner. General Board of Discipleship, Nashville, TN, 2004.

Our Help in Ages Past, The Black Church's Ministry Among the Elderly, Bobby Joe Saucer with Jean Alicia Elster. Valley Forge, PA: Judson Press, 2005.

Preaching for Adult Conversion and Commitment: Invitation to a Life Transformed, Frank G. Honeycutt. Nashville, TN: Abingdon Press, 2004.

Preaching to the Black Middle Class: Words of Challenge, Words of Hope, Marvin A. McMickle. Valley Forge, PA: Judson Press, 2000.

Shoulder to Shoulder: Strengthening Your Church by Supporting Your Pastor, Dan Reiland. Nashville, TN: Thomas Nelson Inc., 1997.

Soul at Work: Spiritual Leadership in Organizations, Margaret Benefiel. New York: Church Publishing, Inc., 2005.

The Empowerment Church: Speaking a New Language for Church Growth, Carlyle Fielding Stewart III. Nashville, TN: Abingdon Press, 2001.

The Purpose Driven Church: Growth Without Compromising Your Message and Mission, Rick Warren. Grand Rapids, MI: Zondervan, 1995.

The Spiritual Leader's Guide to Self Care, Rochelle Melander and Harold Eppley, The Alban Institute, 2002.

The 21 Irrefutable Laws of Leadership: Follow Them and People Will Follow You, John C. Maxwell. Nashville, TN: Thomas Nelson Inc., 1998.

The 21 Most Powerful Minutes in a Leader's Day: Revitalize Your Spirit and Empower Your Leadership, John C. Maxwell. Nashville, TN: Thomas Nelson Inc., 2000.

The Web of Women's Leadership: Recasting Congregational Ministry, Susan Willhauck and Jacqulyn Thorpe. Nashville, TN: Abingdon Press, 2001.

Thirty Days to Confident Leadership, Bobb Biehl. Nashville, TN: Broadman and Holman Publishers, 1998.

Together We Pray: A Prayer Book for Families, J. Bradley Wigger. Atlanta, GA: Chalice Press, 2005.

Twelve Dynamic Shifts for Transforming Your Church, E. Stanley Ott. Grand Rapids, MI: Wm. B. Eerdmans Publishing Co., 2002.

Words That Work: It's Not What You Say, It's What People Hear, Frank Luntz. New York: Hyperion, 2007.

Zion Still Sings! For Every Generation. Nashville, TN: Abingdon Press, 2007.

NOTES

1. Vance Ross, telephone conversation in Atlanta, GA, March 2007.
2. Robert P. Gardner, telephone conversation in Paris, TN, March 2007.
3. Marvin A. McMickle, *Preaching to the Black Middle Class: Words of Challenge, Words of Hope* (Valley Forge, PA: Judson Press, 2000), xi.
4. General Board of Discipleship, "Fifty Characteristics of Disciple-Making Con-

gregations" (by Dean McIntyre), www.gbod.org, 2004; http:// www.umcworship.org. Used by permission.

5. Johnnetta B. Cole, Last Word: "Six Steps to Effective Leadership," *Black Issues in Higher Education*, October 24, 2002, 146.

6. Carlyle Fielding Stewart III, *The Empowerment Church* (Nashville: Abingdon Press, 2001), 61.

7. William M. Easum and Thomas G. Bandy, *Growing Spiritual Redwoods* (Nashville: Abingdon Press, 1997), 127.

8. Rick Warren, *The Purpose Driven Church: Growth Without Compromising Your Message and Mission* (Grand Rapids, Mich.: Zondervan, 1995), 365–366.

9. Ibid., 368–369.

10. Dan Reiland, *Shoulder to Shoulder: Strengthening Your Church by Supporting Your Pastor* (Nashville: Thomas Nelson Inc., 1997), 49–53.

11. Robert Lewis, Wayne Cordeiro, Warren Bird, *Culture Shift: Transforming Your Church From the Inside Out* (San Francisco, CA: JosseyBass, 2005), xxi.

12. Ibid., 3.

13. Warren, inside dust jacket.

14. General Board of Discipleship, gbod.org.

CHAPTER FIVE

SUCH A GREAT CLOUD OF WITNESSES: EVANGELISTICALLY VITAL CHURCHES

F. Douglas Powe, Jr.

We live in a society that often seeks to resolve problems with "five easy step" programs. Lose thirty pounds in five weeks by following this special diet that guarantees results. You can achieve financial success in five easy steps if you follow this investment plan. I am not going to suggest these programs do not work for anyone, but the reality is life is more complicated than solving most issues in five easy steps. The same reality is true for congregations seeking to become evangelistically vital in their communities. No one congregation can copy another and expect the same results, but congregations can learn from the "great cloud of witnesses" some characteristics of evangelistically vital ministries.

What does it mean to be an evangelistically vital church? Many African American Methodist congregations (this issue is not limited to race) have been wrestling with this question since the inception of SBC21. Although one chapter cannot exhaustively describe what evangelistically vital churches look like, the work of SBC21 makes it possible to communicate certain theological and practical characteristics of these churches. This chapter describes how leadership, worship, envisioning, acting propheti-cally, faith formation, and outreach when viewed evangelistically can cre-ate a vital church that not only flourishes in a community, but also is involved in transforming the community. At the heart of this transforma-tion is the Wesleyan notion of personal and social holiness. Wesley's idea of holiness can be described as being transformed into the image of Christ. One way to portray personal and social holiness is the ability of some con-gregations to help members and their surrounding community to experi-ence transformation into full humanity. These churches are actively engaged in not only helping individuals to form a relationship with Christ, but through social activism (often in the form of social justice) these churches are bringing Christ to the community. Learning from such a great cloud of witnesses what it means to be an evangelistically vital church can only strengthen our understanding of holistic ministry.

Three examples of congregations that are evangelistically vital, but are not mega churches[1] are Saint John's UMC in Houston, Texas, Emory UMC in Washington, and Mt. Calvary UMC in Wichita Falls. These con-gregations, as chapter 2 discusses, are evangelistically vital because they are being transformed as bodies of Christ while seeking to transform the community in which they reside. The double movement of a congrega-tion being transformed while transforming the community in which they reside gets to the heart of embodying personal and social holiness. One way to talk about this double movement both theologically and practically is the Pauline trinity of faith, hope, and love. Evangelistically vital con-gregations like Saint John's, Emory, and Mt. Calvary are forming and in some cases reforming those inside and outside of the congregation by help-ing them to be shaped in the faith, participate in hope, and to live out the love of God and neighbor.

FAITH

A common question many pastors ask is, "Where should I begin in trans-forming my congregation?" Answering this question without falling into the trap of developing a five-step program usually ends up frustrating many pastors because they want straightforward practical solutions and trying to get them to reflect upon their contextual situation is sometimes difficult. One place where church leaders and those committed to the academy often agree is on the need for a better understanding of faith by everyone in the church. This does not mean simply repeating Hebrews 11:1 and thinking that should be the end of the conversation. The danger of simply repeating the Hebrews text without further conversation lends itself to two opposite extremes. At one extreme are those individuals who interpret the text to mean believing with one's heart will make something a reality. This type of faith is dangerous because it may never move from a form of inactive spirituality to actively participating in God's work. At the other end of the spectrum are those individuals who interpret the text to mean a type of intellectual assent to the unseen. The danger of this extreme is faith gets subsumed under reason and is reinterpreted into a scientific way of knowing.

One of the reasons that St. John's, Emory and Mt. Calvary are evangelistically vital congregations is their ability to broaden and deepen their understanding of faith. By using Wesleyan language these congregations are able to help parishioners understand the importance of "head and heart" faith. Hal Knight describes the Wesleyan synthesis between head and heart in the following manner: "It is faith that enables us to encounter God as a real and active presence in our lives and world. Faith, then, is more than believing that there is a God—it is knowing God, in some ways as you would know another person."[2] Knight's point is, we cannot choose to simply stop at believing God exists, we must truly know God.

In addition to this Wesleyan understanding of faith, vital congregations must be aware of the social implications of faith. By social implications I mean the importance of faith in addressing the very structures of society. James Cone connects the social aspect of faith to the incarnation:

> The incarnation connects faith with life and work. By becoming human in Jesus, God connects faith with the social, political, and economic conditions of people and establishes the theological conclusions that we cannot be faithful to the Creator without receiving the political command to structure creation according to freedom.[3]

Cone adds to this Wesley understanding of faith by reinterpreting its meaning into an African American context. Faith is more than an individual belief in Jesus the Christ. It has political, economical, and other social implications when Christians begin restructuring society in a manner that moves toward being fully human. The Wesley synthesis of head and heart gets translated into congregations participating in the transformation of societal structures that are oppressing people.

Mt. Calvary's work with the homeless is an example of faith taking on a social dimension.[4] This church moved from strictly professing about faith to "incarnating" their faith in the community. Mt. Calvary is participating in the work of helping those in the community to experience fully human lives by broadening their understanding of what it means to be faithful. The members of Mt. Calvary no longer perceive faith as individualistic and having no social implications. I am not suggesting that every congregation get involved in some form of homeless ministry, but for Mt. Calvary this particular ministry was transformational for individuals in the congregation and for those in the community. Their embodiment of personal and social holiness changed the ethos of the congregation. The question is, "What can we learn from Mt. Calvary and other witnesses who are broadening and deepening their understanding of faith?"

Leadership

If the goal is for congregations to embody personal and social faith as described in the previous paragraphs, what type of leadership is necessary towards this end. Robert Franklin, using the work of James MacGregor Burns, argues there are two types of leaders and one is more helpful than the other for most congregations. He writes:

> Transactional leadership establishes temporary contact with people for the purpose of exchanging valued things (jobs for votes, goods for money, or hospitality for a listening ear). Transformational leadership engages with others so that the leader and followers "raise one another to higher levels of motivation and morality."[5]

Obviously, Franklin is proposing transformational leadership is more helpful than transactional leaders in making a substantial difference in a congregation. Transactional leaders usually are not concerned with synthesizing the head and the heart. Their focus is on the quick fix (the five-step program) and receiving some form of measurable valuable. Transformational leaders, however, are more sensitive to helping a congregation to embody personal and social holiness. The goal is not some measurable form of value, but to be in relationship with others on the journey toward personal and communal transformation.

Franklin outlines several attributes that he perceives as helpful characteristics of a transformational leader. I will highlight three of the attributes he discusses that relate to what it means for leaders of evangelistically vital churches to broaden and deepen the faith of their congregation. First, Franklin describes what he calls an anointed spiritual guide who helps to mediate encounters with the holy.[6] This can be done through spoken word or silence, but it also means knowing when to get out of the way.[7] A leader is not someone who has to be in control of every situation and understands the importance of allowing others to be heard and to lead in certain situations.

Second, there are grassroots intellectuals, who are not only conversant in ecclesial language, but also are knowledgeable about the community in which they reside. Franklin likens this person to the early slave preacher who was knowledgeable about events both inside and outside of the "church walls."[8] The ability to lead in this manner reaffirms the need for both "head and heart" faith and not settling for one in opposition to the other. This type of leader must make sure the wall between the church and community comes down. If the church simply believes this will occur, then they are not taking any concrete actions. A leader who simply talks (intellectualizes) with those outside of the church about the idea of God is not helping to connect the community to the church.

Third, cultural celebrants embrace our African heritage and see it as a way of enriching "our personal and collective lives today."[9] This does not mean continuing to rehearse rituals that need changing or uncritically looking at structural issues like sexism that are a part of the fabric of the African American community. It does mean transmitting some of the values to future generations that helped us to survive and make a way out of no way from the times of slavery. This type of leadership requires discerning how to maintain important African traditions while not excluding ourselves from others.[10]

Certainly there are other characteristics that can be added to the three I have highlighted in this chapter, but leaders who are able to embody these three will help to both deepen and broaden the faith of their members. For example, Rudy Rasmus who with his wife Juanita is copastor of St. John's UMC, changed his attire to blue jeans and sneakers to match those in the community and moved his congregation to a place where attire was no longer a distraction.[11] He visually lived out what it meant to embody a "barrier free" worship experience for current parishioners and those coming into service from the community.[12] The church critically assessed an African American tradition about appropriate attire as an indicator of someone's faith and discerned for their community this barrier needed to be removed. The "simple" act of changing attire was evangelistically important for St. John's because it reconnected the congregation to the community in ways that programmatic efforts could not.

Worship

For many African Americans and Christians in general, worship is still the central place where faith formation occurs. Carlyle Fielding Stewart III suggests one question asked by many seeking a church home is, "Does the worship service meet the deeper yearnings of my spirit?"[13] How someone responds to this question will vary depending on who is answering, but the fact that people are looking for a worship service that helps them on their faith journey is important. Evangelistically vital churches are not homogenous in how they help individuals to live out personal and social holiness. Yet to some extent a commonality among most evangelistically vital congregations is their effort to be invitational.

Stewart claims congregations, ". . . must invite them [people] to belong to the community of faith by encouraging them to engage in critical reflection upon the meaning and purpose of the possibilities of life in that community."[14] This is a faith issue because evangelistically vital congregations do not lose sight of the ideal that the mission of God means existing for other people. Some congregations forget about the big picture and fall into the trap of existing for themselves. Faith gets lived out in a self-serving way that feeds into a members only mentality.[15] Lost is a true Wesleyan understanding of personal and social holiness that pushes individuals to move beyond their own particularities by opening themselves up to others.

If worship becomes a place that just reinforces a members only mentality then it ceases to be a place where one's faith can be transformed. Stewart tells the story of a parishioner unwilling to give up her seat to a visitor and "blessed the pastor out" for suggesting she should give up her seat.[16] The idea that someone owns a seat or that certain areas are reserved for special members point to deeper issues in a congregation. An inviting congregation is a place where members should want to give up their seat so that someone can sit there and worship. Helping congregations to understand the importance of being invitational is not a programmatic issue, but is about changing the very fabric of the way individuals understand what it means to be faithful to God's mission.

It seems a part of the success of Emory UMC was it thought about worship differently. Emory got more people involved in the service and changed the service to reflect a style that was more conducive to those attending. The worship became more invitational not only in tone, but the joy of those worshipping became contagious to visitors. For Emory worship is an important place for faith development because it allows participation by parishioners, and it is where visitors begin their journey with this congregation. Worship is not the end of the journey because the expectation is parishioners will get involved in other faith formation opportunities that extend beyond the four walls of the church.[17] If Emory did not offer an invitational worship experience, then many would never continue the journey to broaden and deepen their faith formation.

Vital Statistics

In some ways we are a society that is attracted to statistics that provide evidence for claims being made. While vital statistics (stats) are important in some instances, we can also think about making claims in different forms. The claims that I am suggesting are important are those that help us to envision the great cloud of witnesses who continues to share with us. These witnesses help us to envision faith as a synthesis between the head and the heart with a strong emphasis on socially acting. Stephanie Mitchem captures this ideal in talking about faith for African American women, but her comments have relevance for the entire Black community. She claims:

> Faith, for black women, becomes a self-defining center that resists socially constructed stereotypes. "God is able" is both a battle cry and a statement of faith. The development of black women's faith is not merely a response to social conditions and is not a form of denial. Faith can provide the alternative space in which black women become self-empowered. Faith in this framework has the cultural groundings of the black community and black women's networks, but it involves a lifelong process of spiritual maturation.[18]

Mitchem's vision of faith speaks to the head and heart synthesis so important to the Wesleyan tradition, and it maintains the importance of social action, which is the life stream of the African American community. Evangelistically vital congregations are not those who simply respond to social conditions, and it is not those living in denial of such conditions,[19] but are those congregations participating in broadening their understanding of faith through creative leadership and invitational worship. These congregations live out their faith in ways that continue to transform their members and the communities in which they reside.

Hope

Some may argue that defining or describing hope is easier than working with the concept of faith. In some ways these individuals are right because the meaning of hope has more of a uniform understanding in our culture than faith. In thinking theologically about the idea of hope, however, I am not convinced it is any easier to grasp than faith. Certainly hope has a futuristic bent to it that speaks to something we seek that is not currently present. As Christians, however, hope is not simply seeking, but requires our participating in creating that future.

Two extremes that usually shape the way we think about hope are certainty with no need for participation or participating to the point of focusing only on good works.[20] Those who advocate for the former usually argue Christ has set the future and nothing we do influences history. Those who advocate for the latter usually argue we (as individuals) must live a certain moral life if our future is going to be set. Neither of these perspectives are entirely wrong, but a more nuanced understanding of hope moves between these two extremes and suggests we live in the already, but not yet. We live knowing what Jesus the Christ has done and that the culmination of God's action in history is yet to come. In the meantime and in between times we are called to live lives that participate in God's renewal or transformation of society. This means what we do is important, but it also means recognizing we do not ultimately control the future.

Like faith, hope also informs how we think about personal and social holiness. Our hope is shaped in communities, but often is lived out in different ways by individuals in communities. As Wesleyans we are called to mirror the love, mercy and justice of God to others as we recover the moral image.[21] The recovery of the moral image of God enables us to mirror to others what we should be moving towards in the "not yet." This understanding of hope has both personal and social implications. Evangelistically vital congregations help their members and the community to make sure human mirrors are accessible both for reflecting and viewing.

Cone adds to this Wesleyan understanding of hope an emphasis on transforming social structures that are oppressive to African Americans. Cone argues that because the existing structures in society are so complex and powerful, trying to destroy them is difficult.[22] Hope is necessary if we are going to continue to struggle without falling prey to despair. For Cone, the fact that Jesus the Christ died and was resurrected in three days should always be a source of hope for African Americans. The time between death and resurrection probably seemed like an eternity to Jesus' followers, similarly for some congregations facing or fighting oppressive structures it often feels like an eternity. The good news is when resurrection occurs the old structures start to get dismantled as something new is being formed. Evangelistically vital congregations are able to not fall prey to despair in the time between death and resurrection.

Vision

Evangelistically vital congregations understand the importance of a shared vision that moves toward personal and social holiness. Many churches spend a lot of energy and time developing mission statements, but do not develop a shared vision that parishioners can participate in as they move toward holiness. Roger Swanson and Shirley Clement distinguish between a vision and a church mission in the following way:

> There is a difference between a mission and a vision. King's "dream" was really a visionary statement. One of the distinguishing characteristics of a true leader is the ability to articulate and to promote vision. . . . A mission marks the boundaries of work. A mission rarely, however, sounds the trumpet to march forward.[23]

The example of King's "I have a Dream" speech is a helpful reference for understanding what we mean by vision. The power of that particular speech as Swanson and Clement point out is it sounded a trumpet inviting people to march forward toward a new future.[24]

A vision invites parishioners to move forward toward something new that participates in God's coming reign. Stewart hones in on the important connection between a vision and the coming reign of God. He writes:

> The prophetic dimensions of Jesus' mission and ministry were based upon visions of a new heaven and a new earth. His entire focus was on building the kingdom of God in the here and now, and preparing people for its coming. It is essential to have an understanding of what life can be, in order to bring the vision into reality.[25]

Connecting one's vision to the coming reign of God enables Christians to participate in bringing the reign into fruition, and sets an ideal for what it is the church and society are moving toward. Returning to the example of King's "I Have a Dream" speech, it articulated a vision that Blacks and Whites could participate in together. The speech was ultimately grounded in a vision of the coming reign of God towards which King hoped the church and society were moving. A vision of helping those disenfranchised to experience full humanity and not the oppressive structures currently defining their lives.

How do evangelistically vital congregations shape their visions? The answers vary depending on context and resources. Two common elements that many evangelistic congregations share: (1) the vision is big enough to be a dream and (2) realistic enough to be inviting. A biblical example is helpful in this case from the book of Nehemiah. Nehemiah envisions rebuilding the Jerusalem wall, which had been destroyed when some of the Israelites were taken into captivity and only a remnant remained in Israel.[26] This is a big vision and one that many Israelites probably dreamed about during the time the wall was destroyed. Yet, Nehemiah's vision is realistic because he knew that the community could rebuild the wall by working together. Nehemiah was also aware not everyone would support the vision and some would attempt to derail it. Nehemiah did not let those in opposition to him stop his work or to squash the hopes of those who bought into his dream from the community. The community was empowered by Nehemiah's vision and acted to make the vision a reality.[27]

The social transformation inherent in the text through the rebuilding of the wall is another important component to the Nehemiah text. Many of the Israelites had lost hope and the rebuilding of the wall symbolized a restoration into nationhood. Even before the project was finished and parts of the wall were rebuilt, the community started experiencing transformation as the vision became more of a reality. The point is the Israelites did not have to wait until the project was finished to experience social transformation; it happened as a part of the process.

St. John's UMC did not rebuild the Jerusalem wall, but they did engender hope in the church and surrounding area by turning the parsonage into a community facility.[28] The vision was to create a community facility that could "serve the homeless, hungry and unemployed."[29] St. John's went a step further and served the homeless the meals in their sanctuary.[30] How many churches have a vision to turn the parsonage into a community facility? Even more radical, "How many churches are willing to use their sanctuary as a place to feed the hungry?" Because the homeless began to feel at home in the sanctuary some of those who were served started attending service.

St. John's was able to develop a vision that not only transformed the congregation, but also the community in which they resided. The vision was big enough to be a dream, but realistic enough to be inviting to those inside and outside of the church. St. John's was able to dismantle some of the oppressive structures facing individuals within that church and community. Transforming the institutional practices that the homeless and others experienced in that community helped them to move toward full humanity in ways those inside and outside of the church never imagined.

Evangelistically vital churches find ways to make their visions big enough to include the community, but inclusive enough to secure the participation of current members. St. John's vision was evangelistic because it helped people to move towards full humanity by dismantling some of the institutional structures oppressing them. It was also evangelistic in the way that St. John's creatively used the sanctuary as a welcoming and sacred space. St. John's lived out what it means to help individuals to grow in personal and social holiness. Although other churches cannot copy exactly what St. John's did, St. John's is a witness to how developing a vision grounded in hope can be evangelistic and change social situations.

Prophetic

Evangelistically vital churches are called to be prophetic and in many instances countercultural. The term prophetic often means different things depending on who is defining it in our society. For many African Americans, King offers a way to understand this idea of the prophetic that connects churches and communities together.[31] King's effort to bring America together during the turbulent Civil Rights Movement was grounded in the idea of prophetic ministry. Franklin encapsulates King's idea of prophetic ministry in the following quote:

> For King, African-American prophetic Christianity was rooted in a biblical faith that affirmed the original goodness and divine sovereignty over creation. In light of human sinfulness, however, religion and ethics bore the ongoing task of seeking to reconcile and restore creation to its intended excellence. By asserting this courageously, King challenged the folk beliefs of many black churches and much southern Protestantism, which devalued life in this cruel world and preoccupied themselves with the "other world." He insisted that looking away from this world in anxious embrace of the next was not an authentically Christian or biblically defensible option in the face of human suffering. He called them to work faithfully and hopefully in order to change people's souls as well as their environmental conditions so that the new souls might be nurtured by new social structures.[32]

Franklin articulates King's hope that a prophetic understanding of ministry does not fall into the either/or trap of the soul against the body. A prophetic understanding of ministry values both the soul and the body as it seeks to reconcile the world back to God. In Wesleyan language, King argues social holiness is just as important as personal holiness and focusing on one side against the other can lead to dysfunctional ministry. Inherent to the idea of the prophetic for King is appropriating the tension between the temporal and the eternal.[33]

The challenge for evangelistically vital churches appropriating the tension between the temporal and the eternal means knowing how to be countercultural while still connecting to the community. The tendency is either to adapt the ways of the culture without question so that it becomes difficult to distinguish between the church and the culture or to become so "holy" that those in the world get demonized because they are not like "us" in the church. Navigating between these poles requires an understanding of the cultural climate in which the church operates, and a willingness to maintain the countercultural emphasis of the prophetic tradition in the Bible.

Emory UMC is able to navigate between the two poles because it stays culturally relevant while being countercultural. The idea of being culturally relevant and countercultural at the same time seems like an oxymoron. Is Emory buying into the culture to some extent? The answer is yes, but not to the extent that the church has nothing to say back to the culture. Emory is culturally relevant when it comes to stylistic issues like genre of music, liturgical dance, and other such matters.[34] Emory is countercultural in its expectation for what it means to help people live fully human lives. This congregation's prophetic edge calls into question structures disabling individuals into growing into the likeness of Christ.

Emory dwindled down to nine parishioners at one time and was getting ready to become part of a two-point charge.[35] The congregation could have looked inward and taken the attitude we need to "save" our church. By continuing to look for ministry opportunities outside of the church (example, health and welfare),[36] Emory avoided falling into a dualism that ignored the surrounding community and focusing only on the souls of believers (within the congregation). Emory's involvement in prison, health and welfare, educational ministries helped to bridge the temporal versus eternal dualism that plagues many churches. Emory's evangelistic vitality is grounded in testifying a prophetic word to those not only needing to hear something new, but also needing oppressive social structures challenged. Churches able to testify a prophetic word and to challenge oppressive social structures regardless of their numerical growth will be vital to their communities.

Vital Statistics

Evangelistically vital churches are able to sustain hope even in the most challenging times. These churches understand that an inviting vision and prophetic witness can help those in the congregation and community to think differently about their lives. Thinking about the church as the locus of this type of vision, and prophetic witness means helping individuals live into personal and social holiness. Evangelistically vital churches like Emory do not draw up a blueprint and work on personal holiness one week and social holiness the next. These churches are more organic and understand how personal and social holiness are interconnected usually occurring at the same time in the midst of the journey.

We must be careful, however, about how we think and act out our hope on the journey. There is no guarantee that just because we have hope our church and community will be transformed. It is still the Holy Spirit that transforms lives and structures. In many African American communities where suffering is a part of every day life, it seems cruel to say that hope will not automatically translate into transformation for a particular situation. The truth is it is only by sustaining hope that transformation is possible. This transformation is not formulaic, but a movement toward (w)holiness.[37] It is a movement toward what it means to experience full humanity in the midst of oppressive challenges.

LOVE

Paul encourages us to abide in faith, hope, and love but to always remember love is the greatest of the three (I Corinthians 13:13). Love of God and love of neighbor should be the starting point from which everything else in our Christian lives flow. We are not involved in the community because we are trying to "work" our way into heaven, but out of our genuine love for God and our neighbor. Wesley's understanding of personal and social holiness is grounded in the idea love of God and neighbor.

We must be cautious even in using the language of love of God and neighbor. The challenge for evangelistically vital churches will be not to

131

make love cheap or to make "my gospel" the one way of understanding Christianity.[38] Cheap love often occurs when we put limits on who is our neighbor.[39] In some congregations this gets lived out in class distinctions between those driving into urban churches from the suburbs. The actual makeup of the congregation does not reflect the community in which the church resides. In many of these cases the parishioners make little effort to reach out to those in the community, yet they wonder why no one from the surrounding area attends. This is an example of cheap love because the congregation gathers only for its own benefit and makes little effort to participate in the community.

Cheap love is one challenge some churches face and another is promoting my gospel or trying to control others through the gospel.[40] Returning to the example of the congregation driving into an urban church, but in this case they are involved in the community. They are actively promoting their gospel as the one interpretation of the Bible within the community. Although the church is active in the surrounding area it still has a misinformed understanding of loving one's neighbor because now they are moving away from an openness to God's word and predetermining how individuals in the neighborhood must interpret it.

A Wesleyan model for love of God and neighbor should navigate between these misinformed ways of expressing love. Truly loving God and our neighbor means we are living at the intersection of personal and social holiness. We are learning the habits (acts of piety) that help us to love God as a daily practice and not just on Sunday—prayer, searching the Scriptures, Lord's Supper, fasting and Christian conversation;[41] likewise, we are learning habits (acts of mercy) that help us to love our neighbor in ways that are not cheap or controlling. These (acts of mercy) can include developing covenant groups, testimonial fellowships and visiting the sick.[42] Wesley's emphasis was on developing a relationship with one's neighbor that was meaningful without diminishing the humanity of the other.

Cone further develops our understanding of love by starting with a question: "What does it mean to love the exploited social classes, the dominated people or a marginalized race?"[43] Cone emphasizes the relational component to Wesley's model of love of God and neighbor. Rewording Cone's question within a Wesleyan framework would mean asking, "How do we develop covenant groups or testimonial fellowships with the least in our society?" Answering this question is difficult, but some of our evangelistically vital congregations are doing it. St. John's is doing it by rethinking sacred space and covenanting with those struggling in the community to perceive even the sanctuary as a place where they can gather and eat.

Let me quickly address those who will claim my neighbor may not be marginalized. Certainly some of our churches are in wealthier areas where most of the people look like us and are in our same economic class. These churches, however, may struggle with loving their neighbor because of theology, race, political affiliation, and so forth. We can benefit from Wesley and Cone's pushing us to ask deeper questions about the ways we live out loving God and our neighbor.

Faith Formation

Earlier in the chapter we talked about faith as a category and the importance of avoiding some of the extremes in living faithful lives. At this point I will talk about how we can be shaped in the faith to better live out loving God and our neighbor. Wesley had some strong ideas on the best way for Methodists to live out the love of God and neighbor. As I mentioned at the beginning of this section one of the ways Wesley implores us to do this is by visiting the sick. Wesley writes:

> By the sick, I do not mean only those that keep in their bed, or that are sick in the strictest sense. Rather I would include all such as are in a state of affliction, whether of mind or body; and that whether they are good or bad, whether fear God or not. But is there need of visiting them in person? May we not relieve them at a distance?…The word which we render 'visit,' in its literal acceptation, means, 'to look upon'. And this, you know, cannot be done, unless you are present with them.[44]

I could discuss many ramifications for faith formation from Wesley's quote, but one that is central to Wesley's ministry is being relational. Visiting someone requires physical contact with that individual and not just the sending of resources. The lesson for our congregations is loving our neighbor requires knowing the neighbor. If the church is invisible in a particular neighborhood, then we must begin to ask how the church is relating to its neighbors?

Loving our neighbor also requires an intersection with loving God. Sondra Matthaei helps us to think about this intersection from a Wesleyan perspective. Matthaei suggests that Wesley believed persons do not enter into a work of mercy like visiting the sick thinking that they are doing something on their own accord.[45] It is God who works through us and gives us the strength to do this manner of work.[46] We cannot divorce what we

133

do for our neighbor even in a relational manner from our practices of loving God.

Mt. Calvary UMC started a daycare and after school ministry.[47] This ministry focuses on helping the young people to experience and view life differently. Mt. Calvary figured out a way to be relational in their surrounding community and to help young people to move towards full humanity. This church does not understand this ministry as some great human effort, but it is participating in making God's presence a reality in that community. For Mt. Calvary to fully enrich the lives of the young people it requires practicing the love of God through prayer, and I imagine patience. More importantly, Mt. Calvary has committed to participating in ministry within the neighborhood in a new way, but in a way that is not cheap or controlling. Evangelistically vital congregations live at the intersection of personal and social holiness (love of God and neighbor) while trying to stay open to the work of the Spirit.

Outreach

A lot of material has been written on the false split between social outreach and evangelism. Evangelistically vital congregations usually do not fall into the trap of this dualism. Framing this conversation with Wesley and Cone is another way to help others avoid this dangerous dualism. Integrating the thinking of Wesley and Cone pushes us to live at the intersection of personal and social holiness without negating one for the other. As pointed out in talking about faith formation, living at this intersection also means thinking through what it means to be relational in a given community. One of the reasons many churches suffer from the false dichotomy between social action and evangelism is outreach is divorced from faith formation and simply becomes social action. Churches must learn to love their neighbors in a way that reflects the love of God without being imperialistic.

How can churches build healthy relationships with individuals in the community? I cannot give an exact blueprint because contexts are different, but some characteristics that are helpful to consider include reflecting God's love to others, reporting God's love to others, and allowing others to respond to God's love.[48] Reflecting God's love to others gets back to the idea of mirroring. As Christians we should mirror what it means to love God, and we should mirror God's love to others.[49] One positive result of reflecting God's love to others is those in the community will no longer feel like strangers among us. Stewart tells a story that is helpful in illustrating this point:

One pastor related an experience with a church that had developed a reputation in the community as being cold and uncongenial. Worship services were virtually empty on Sunday, and the church never opened its doors to people in the surrounding area. It was only after the church began to allow community groups to utilize meeting space that a noticeable change in worship attendance occurred. By simply opening its doors and creating a climate of outreach, it experienced growth.[50]

The church was perceived as cold and unloving until it literally opened its doors to the community and reflected a different image of itself and God. By creating a communal space the church was perceived differently by those in the area who had not experienced the church as invitational.

Reporting God's love to others is often more difficult than reflecting it to others. Many of us are willing to reflect God's love to our neighbor, but it seems invasive to actually tell others about God's love.[51] We must be cautious not to impose God's love on others; unfortunately this is the typical picture of evangelism that many have in the United States. When we develop a relationship with others, opportunities arise allowing us to express God's love. Knight and Powe address this issue by suggesting:

Reporting God's love to others is not an attempt on our part to fool, manipulate or force anyone into believing something different. It is instead an unapologetic and honest reporting of how we have experienced God's love and goodness. When God is transforming us it will shine through in ways we cannot imagine and bring us into relationships with individuals we could never imagine.[52]

Reporting God's love to one's neighbor should not be a burden, and it should not be manipulative. As Knight and Powe indicate it often brings us into relationships with others we never would have imagined, and we are often surprised by what occurs in those encounters.

The reporting of God's love is not just about personal holiness; it is about transforming structures. Stewart reports:

One pastor told of his success in simply having town meetings at the church to resolve the problems of crime in the community. The response by community residents was overwhelming. In fact, the meetings were so successful that a task force was developed to take their concerns to the mayor and city council.[53]

Stewart comments further that by the church inviting those in the community to address a problem and showing a willingness to get actively involved, those in the community heard the proclamation from church members differently.[54] Reporting God's love to others is not simply about personal holiness, but is about social holiness and addressing structural concerns in communities. If the church had not been willing to go out and proclaim God's love by opening up a space for the community, then the community would not have been empowered to take their concerns to the mayor. Because of this action some of the people empowered by the church's commitment in the neighborhood joined the church.[55] Evangelistically vital churches are able to make inroads into their surrounding areas because they are willing to report the gospel in such a way that it changes the very ethos of the community.

Possibly the most difficult of the three characteristics I am outlining is allowing others to respond to the Holy Spirit. Knight and Powe claim, "Sometimes as Christians we become so determined to help someone enter into a relationship with Jesus the Christ that we forget the person is not responding to us, but to God."[56] The same holds true for when we are trying to transform oppressive social structures. We participate in God's work, but we are not God. Leaving space for God to work in personal or social situations is important and it reinforces to our neighbor that we do in fact love them. A desire for others to experience God's love can potentially cause us to impose God's will on others instead of allowing the Holy Spirit to work.

All three churches that have been an integral part of this chapter (Emory, Mt. Calvary, and St. John's) had to learn to rely on the Holy Spirit. These churches are evangelistically vital now, but at one time they were struggling like many of our churches. These churches learned how to allow space for God to work while continually participating in bringing about the reign of God. This is the balancing act all churches must face that seek to be vital in their communities. Living at the intersection of personal and social holiness means loving God by being attentive to God's voice. It also means acting on God's voice through reflecting and reporting this love to one's neighbor. This is the challenge for evangelistically vital churches and those who are comfortable living at this intersection are being transformed and participating in the transformation of their communities.

Vital Statistics

Loving God and loving one's neighbor should be at the heart of all of our evangelistic endeavors. Integrating the thinking of Wesley and Cone pushes us to move beyond the false dichotomy of evangelism or social action. Evangelistically vital congregations are trying to help individuals move toward full humanity by reflecting and reporting God's love to them, while seeking to remove oppressive structures that are disempowering those in the community. Evangelistically vital congregations are always aware of the fact that they must allow the Holy Spirit to do the transforming and not impose their desires on others.

Loving God and loving our neighbors is even more important in some African American communities, especially those located in blight areas. Some of the challenges in these blight communities are higher rates of poverty and crime because of various structural issues in society. Churches in these communities are faced with loving neighbors who face life and death situations daily. Robert Franklin is concerned "that African American churches are not as ready as they should be to meet the challenges ahead."[57] Franklin is right about the challenges ahead, but evangelistically vital congregations are ready for the challenges. They are ready not because they are unique or radically different from other churches. They are ready because they are willing to live at the intersection of personal and social holiness opening themselves up to the community so that God can transform lives and structures.

Such a Great Cloud of Witnesses

We do have a great cloud of witnesses that we can learn from and be encouraged by as we seek to help others to live fully human lives. The mandate coming out of the 1996 General Conference starting the Strengthening the Black Church Initiative recognized the importance of this cloud of witnesses. A portion of the mandate reads:

> To offer the United Methodist Church the gift of a transformational model that enables one congregation to share its gift of vitality with other churches wanting to expand their gifts in mission and ministry; and in the process, to revitalize Black congregations and The United Methodist Church.

> The initiative was developed on the principle that resources are already present in many churches and communities that can be shared with other churches and communities. The initiative offers an opportunity for vibrant, growing congregations to provide mentoring for other congregations desiring growth, vitality and transformation.[58]

The biblical idea behind the initiative is to create a great cloud of witnesses that can help other churches think theologically and practically about what it means to be an evangelistically vital congregation. This does not mean congregations are expected to follow an exact map or some five-step program on their way to becoming evangelistically vital. It does mean congregations must learn how to reflect theologically on their ministry and contextual settings.

One of the advantages of using the Pauline trinity of faith, hope, and love is it provides a framework in which congregations can shape their particular ministries differently. Certainly some commonalities exist in our understanding of these categories, and I have suggested some possible polemics we should avoid in working in a particular context. These categories, however, are open enough that a congregation like St. John's can embody faith, hope, and love very differently than Emory. Both congregations are a part of the cloud of witnesses that can help other churches to become more evangelistically vital.

The one common denominator that all of the evangelistically vital churches embody and I am suggesting should be a part of the ethos of any congregation is helping individuals and communities to move toward what it means to be fully human. The Wesleyan focus on personal and social holiness is a way of talking about forming lives within a Christian context to become more human. Cone's focus on challenging oppression facing the least among us is about dismantling systemic structures keeping individuals and communities from becoming fully human. Any church that seeks to become an evangelistically vital congregation has to think critically about what it means to be faithful, to help people participate in hope, and to practice love of God and neighbor as a way of transforming lives and communities toward a different vision of full humanity.

The mandate from the General Conference talks about a cloud of witnesses (my language) giving a gift to The United Methodist Church. If this cloud of witnesses can help churches to think critically about living at the intersection of personal and social holiness so that lives and communities can be transformed, then the whole church would benefit. If this cloud of witnesses can help churches to think critically about the connection between faith formation, participating in a new future, and loving others, then the whole church would benefit. If this cloud of witnesses can help churches to think critically about a Christian vision that moves toward helping people to live more human lives, then the whole church would benefit. Evangelistically vital congregations are not perfect churches, but are churches willing to step outside of the "box" to shape, challenge, and encourage others inside and outside of the church to live their lives more fully.

NOTES

1. I am not speaking out against mega churches or larger congregations who also should be evangelistically vital. My point is that the size of a congregation does not determine whether or not it is a vital church.
2. Hal Knight III, *Eight Life-Enriching Practices of United Methodists* (Nashville: Abingdon Press, 2001), 11.
3. James Cone, *Speaking the Truth: Ecumenism, Liberation, and Black Theology* (Maryknoll, NY: Orbis Books, 1986), 47.
4. EcuFilm, "Legacy of Faith II."
5. Robert M. Franklin, *Another Day's Journey* (Minneapolis, MN: Fortress Press, 1997), 121.
6. Ibid., 122.
7. Ibid.
8. Ibid., 123.
9. Ibid.
10. Ibid., 124
11. St. John's Downtown, "Blueprint Church: St. John's United Methodist Church" (by Christian Washington), August 25, 2002, www.stjohnsdowntown.org.
12. Ibid.
13. Carlyle Fielding Stewart III, *African American Church Growth: 12 Principles for Prophetic Ministry* (Nashville: Abingdon Press, 1994), 56.
14. Ibid., 64
15. Ibid.
16. Ibid.
17. See EmoryUMC.org.
18. Stephanie Y. Mitchem, *Introducing Womanist Theology* (Marynoll, NY: Orbis Books, 2002), 49.
19. Ibid.
20. Knight, *Eight Life Enriching Practices*, 22.
21. Theodore Weber, *Politics in the Order of Salvation* (Nashville: Kingswood Books, 2001), 394.
22. Cone, *Speaking the Truth*, 48.
23. Roger K. Swanson and Shirley F. Clement, *Faith-Sharing Congregation* (Nashville: Abingdon Books, 2002), 86.
24. Ibid.
25. Stewart, *African American Church Growth*, 38.
26. Read the book of Nehemiah for a full account of the story.
27. Stewart, *African American Church Growth*, 37.
28. Washington, "Blue Print Church," 1.
29. Ibid.

30. Ibid.
31. King is not the only way to understand the idea of the prophetic, but he does provide some good insights into this term.
32. Robert M. Franklin, *Liberating Visions: Human Fulfillment and Social Justice in African-American Thought* (Minneapolis, MN: Fortress Press, 1990), 121.
33. Ibid.
34. Strengthening The Black Church, *Life Transformation in the Black Church*, 2004
35. Ibid.
36. EmoryUMC.org.
37. Mitchem, *Womanist Theology*, 111.
38. Hal Knight, III and F. Douglas Powe, *Transforming Evangelism: The Wesleyan Way of Sharing Faith* (Nashville: Discipleship Resources, 2006), 78.
39. Ibid.
40. Ibid.
41. Ibid., 49.
42. Knight, *Eight Life-Enriching Practices of United Methodists*, 29.
43. Cone, *Speaking the Truth*, 46–47.
44. John Wesley, "On Visiting the Sick," *Works 3* (Nashville: Abingdon Press, 1986), par. 1.1, 387.
45. Sondra Matthaei, *Making Disciples: Faith Formation in the Wesleyan Tradition* (Nashville: Abingdon Press, 2000), 158.
46. Ibid.
47. EcuFilm, "Legacy of Faith II."
48. Knight and Powe, *Transforming Evangelism*, 80–84.
49. Ibid.
50. Stewart, *African American Church Growth*, 119–120.
51. Knight and Powe, *Transforming Evangelism*, 83.
52. Ibid., 84.
53. Stewart, *African American Church Growth*, 120.
54. Ibid., 121.
55. Ibid.
56. Knight and Powe, *Transforming Evangelism*, 84–85.
57. Franklin, *Another Day's Journey*, 125.
58. "Strengthening The Black Church For The 21st Century Initiative," 2000 General Conference, 2.

CHAPTER SIX

THE GIFT: THE MISSION, THE MODEL, AND THE MESSAGE

Fred Smith, Jr.

In Christ God was reconciling the world to himself. We are ambassadors for Christ, since God is making his appeal through us; we entreat you on behalf of Christ, be reconciled to God.

(II Corinthians 5:19, 20)

I. THE MISSION: AMBASSADORS OF THE BELOVED COMMUNITY IN THE TWENTY-FIRST CENTURY

The goal of SBC21 is the revitalization of the Black Church for ministry. Yet, what has evolved is a gift, offering a model that could serve as a catalyst for revival and revitalization for the whole denomination. Decline in membership, resources, and spiritual vitality are not just problems faced by many Black churches. The United Methodist denomination as a whole is experiencing decline. As expressed in earlier chapters, SBC21 has created a model that seeks to reverse these trends by developing a process of congregational discipling in five areas: leadership, worship, faith formation, outreach, and planning. This chapter will explore the lessons learned and the insights achieved by SBC21 congregations in these five transformative practices.

A transformative practice is a means by which a congregation is able to change itself, members, and community according to the word (logos) of God. In this case the focus is on the congregation itself. The transformation is from impending death to vitality and life found in spiritual rebirth. First, the practice of spiritual leadership, by both clergy and lay, is the single most important factor for strengthening and transforming the church. Leadership, which is rarely requested as a training event, is difficult to teach; it must be demonstrated. The evaluations of the SBC21 training events positively comment on the strong leadership demonstrated by the CRCs. The second practice, worship, is the central function and work of the congregation. In fact, the vitality of a congregation is measured by its worshipping life. Worship training events were the most requested by PCs. Third, forming congregants in the Christian faith through discipleship is the mission of the church. Many participants commented on the post-evaluations that the CRCs were an excellent source of curricular resources and pedagogies for discipleship. Fourth, the practice of reaching out to the "least of these" is also a primary responsibility of vital congregations. Outreach (along with worship) is the most outstanding strength of most CRCs. Also, PCs were most likely to implement outreach after the training event. Last, like leadership, the practice of planning is rarely requested and its value is best demonstrated. One of the most consistent comments PCs made on the post-evaluation was appreciation for how well the events were planned.

In order to share these learnings and insights with the larger church, we must first assess the SBC21 training events. Our experience strongly supports the discipling relationship created by the pairing and mentoring of CRCs and PCs as a sustainable method of revitalization and revival. The central question, however, is how The United Methodist Church can use this model for revival and the revitalization of all congregations? SBC21's greatest gift may not be just a model but an insight. The centrality of hope in Christ for revival is the ultimate source of congregational vitality.

The first submission of the SBC21 Initiative expressed this central hope at the 1996 General Conference: "Broken covenant and broken people are not powerful enough to prevent the redemptive love of God from reclaiming human lives for community. It, therefore, is by and through Jesus Christ, that we are called to the unity of the beloved community." This statement implies something more than vital congregations as an end in themselves, but instead it is a calling toward wholeness via unity of the Beloved Community. The insight derived from the brokenness of centuries of slavery, lynching, and racial discrimination is a hope that is centered in Jesus Christ alone. The centrality of the hope in Christ for the healing of broken people and the mending of broken covenants is the means by which revival and revitalization will ultimately come. This vision of wholeness and call to unity of the Beloved Community will be the pathway for the remaking of The United Methodist Church by the reconciling power of the redemptive love of God through the Cross of Jesus Christ.

As we have seen in earlier chapters, the Black Methodist church was born in response to a broken covenant of Christian fellowship. Black Methodists for centuries have and do experience the historical brokenness as a result of slavery and Jim Crow as well the daily brokenness caused by racism. However, it is the broken covenant of Christ's commandment to love one another as he has loved us (John 13:34) that is most egregious to a people of faith. Race prejudice and bigotry in the church are shattering to the witness of Christ in the world. The covenant that was broken is the new covenant and final prayer of Christ (John 13:34-35, John 17: 20-23). The results of this brokenness have so warped the church that Sunday morning at 11:00 a.m. is still the most segregated hour in America. Doing ministry within a predominantly White denomination that itself has participated in the broken covenant of racial segregation and slavery (Methodist Church South and Central Jurisdiction), contributes to the lack of strength in Black churches.

Black United Methodists suffer from the malady of double-consciousness. In *The Souls of Black Folks* Dubois characterizes this situation as a "peculiar sensation":

> It is a peculiar sensation, this double-consciousness, this sense of always looking at one's self through the eyes of others, of measuring one's soul by the tape of a world that looks on in amused contempt and pity. One ever feels his two-ness—an American, a Negro; two souls, two thoughts, two unreconciled strivings; two warring ideals in one dark body, whose dogged strength alone keeps it from being torn asunder.[1]

This "peculiar sensation" is a way of knowing and seeing as if from behind a veil. Blacks in The United Methodist Church have always been conscious of their place as a minority in a majority denomination. Double-consciousness divides the Black United Methodist's Christian identity from its racial identity within his or her own denomination. This brokenness leads to a lack of focus and saps a person's energy to do ministry in many cases. Often this double consciousness compromises the Black Methodists' Christian witness in their own community that views this double-consciousness as a weakness in the one institution that they have come to depend on for strength. Yet, it is the dogged strength of our hope in Christ that has kept Black Methodists and The United Methodist Church from being torn asunder.

It was out of the power of this brokenness that *Songs of Zion* was composed by people broken by slavery and the struggle for freedom. Twenty-five years ago, a group of African American United Methodists felt called to bring "songs of the soul and soil" from the Black church into the mainline hymnal, *Songs of Zion*.[2] It was the power of the brokenness of racial discrimination that built institutions to sustain the social progress of a people. These institutions included higher education, public schools, funeral homes, businesses, transportation, and even churches. This same brokenness of double consciousness fueled by spiritual impulses of the centrality of hope in Christ, created political and social movements organized to fight for the civil rights of broken people. This power also gave birth to the Black Church; born out of insult and the humiliation of a broken covenant by those White brothers and sisters who claimed to be children of God.

"The power of broken covenant and broken people is not powerful enough to prevent the redemptive love of God from reclaiming human lives for community." What is clear is that only God can heal our brokenness and forgive our sins against one another because our hope is centered in Christ. Christ's healing of our brokenness often takes place in spite of our best effort to hold on to our victimization. Despite our desire to perpetuate patterns of behavior and social inactions to which we have grown accustomed, God is creating a new thing in our midst. Through Jesus Christ and his death and resurrection, God calls us into the unity of the Beloved Community.

According to Martin Luther King Jr., the Beloved Community is the call of Jesus Christ for a people broken by years of legal segregation, violent repression, economic exploitation, and miseducation. King sought to redeem the soul of a nation that has broken the promise of both democracy and Christianity to people of African descent. Through a vision of the reign of God's Redemptive Love in the Beloved Community, SBC21 shares the dream of Dr. Martin Luther King Jr. Many of the clergy and laity of the CRCs and PCs, who in their brokenness, see themselves as heralds of God's call to overcome this brokenness.

Healing broken people and mending broken covenants is the substance of the gift to the wider church. Strong spiritual leadership, vibrant worship, mature faith formation, transformative outreach and effective planning are the core transformative practices of vital congregations. A vision of wholeness of the Beloved Community is the calling and mission for vital congregations of any kind that is centered in a hope in Christ.

As we look ahead to the next phase of SBC21, increasingly it will become apparent that to strengthen the Black Church is not possible without strengthening the whole church of Jesus Christ. The mission that shapes the church is to reclaim human lives for community by sharing the redemptive love of Christ. Congregations are called into being for mission, and it is only as the mission is revitalized that congregations are made vital. Congregations shaped by the mission of Christ become conduits of the love of God to reclaim human lives for the Beloved Community.

The gift of the SBC21 is a concrete model for revitalizing the mission and shaping congregations. While vitality is important, it is not the congregation's main calling. All Christian congregations are commanded to love and are called into unity in Jesus Christ. Christ has broken down the dividing wall of hostility (Ephesians 2:14). Thus, we proclaim: "Broken covenants and broken people are not powerful enough to prevent *the redemptive love of God from reclaiming human lives for community. It, therefore, is by and through Jesus Christ, that we are called to the unity of the Beloved Community.*"

The gift of SBC21, then, is both the mission and model. A mission centered in a hope in Christ shapes vital congregations. Also, the congregation to congregations' discipleship model strengthens the aforementioned five core transformative practices (leadership, worship, community outreach, faith formation, and planning). Our task then is to assess the utility of model for The United Methodist Church at large and to confess and proclaim our hope in Christ for the healing of our brokenness.

II. THE MODEL: LESSONS, INSIGHTS, AND IMPLICATIONS

The SBC21 model can strengthen any church. The key is outstanding leadership found in lay and clergy Black United Methodists. Therefore, it is important that some of these leaders share their experiences. In this section pastors who have labored to make SBC21 an initiative will elaborate on their experiences in three different areas: (1) Lessons Learned – Rudy Rasmus of St. John's UMC in Houston; (2) Insights Gained – Joseph Daniels of Emory UMC in Washington, D.C.; (3) Implications for the Future – Adrienne Terry of St. Matthews UMC in Baltimore. By candidly sharing their insights, these leaders will demonstrate the kind of gift SBC21 can be for The United Methodist Church.

LESSONS LEARNED

St. John's was one of the original CRCs. Rudy Rasmus states, "One of our greatest mistakes was to use another church's framework to teach others. We had to learn to trust our own experience both good and bad." Following are other eight essential lessons learned.

1. The Benefits of Partner Congregations

One key lesson learned was that the CRC and the PC benefited from this mentoring model. It was not a one-way street. CRCs often came to realize that they learned as much about themselves as they taught others according to Rev. Rasmus: "We were experiencing growth at the time. We were literally becoming a different church after every five hundred new members. We were learning what to do while we were teaching others what to do. Being a Congregation Resource Center was a validation of our congregation's ministry."

Once CRCs understand they have something to teach others that can help them serve Christ, it boosts the confidence of the host congregation. It also leads to improved practice as CRCs receive feedback from PCs about their experience. Thus, all the congregations involved in SBC21 are truly partners in learning.

2. The Effectiveness of a Serious Congregation

Many PCs were not serious about learning. Often they were only interested in a free trip. We found it was more effective to invite PCs that were serious about learning from the CRC. According to Rev. Rasmus, "Many churches don't grow because the people leading them and the people in them have never seen a church grow. Some churches just are not going to grow because people do not want to grow. We need to put the money on churches with the greatest opportunity. We must look for bright spots. A determination has to be made, whether churches are serious about growing. Only people on the pew can answer that question."

One of the most painful things we learned was that not all congregations want to be vital or to grow. One of the greatest challenges facing SBC21 is to develop a means to assess a congregation's readiness for a mentoring relationship with a CRC. Rev. Rasmus and St. John's began by searching out those who had a heart to serve the poor as a litmus test. It will be important for SBC21 to develop an assessment tool or process, beyond the present criteria. An invitation only system probably will not work but should be considered along with a referral program.

3. A Focus on Core Competences

We learned to focus our efforts on what we do well. We discovered that focusing on our core competences, rather than all the categories was more effective. Matching core competences in similar contexts is the key to matching experiences and expectations.

All CRCs are not equally able to teach all five of the transformative practices. Likewise, PCs come to training events with different needs and expectations. When each CRC is expected to provide training in each of the five transformative practices and every PC receives the same training, often neither leaves the training event satisfied that it was time well spent. It would be more efficient to bring together multiple CRCs with effective ministries and the same transformative practices. These ministries can join PCs with similar experiences and ministry contexts in one setting to learn from each other. They must also share what has not worked as well as what has worked. Thus CRCs can focus on teaching from its core competency and the PCs can receive the training that matches their perceived needs.

4. Learnings from Other Ethnic Groups

One weakness of SBC21 is that it draws on only a fragment of the church's resources. It appears to accommodate the brokenness in our denomination and our nation as a whole, with a seeming premise that Black churches can only learn from other Black churches. We need to encourage people to allow ministry to take place regardless of ethnic origins. While it is true that there are cultural differences between ethnic groups that impact our ministry practices, it is also true that these differences exist within Black churches as well. Another limitation is not reaching out to other denominations. At the very least SBC21 could have included Pan-

Methodist CRCs and PCs. The key to the success of this model as gift to the church will be its ability to take this next important step. That is, moving beyond race and denominationalism in order to strengthen all churches.

5. Regional Considerations for CRCs

When matching CRCs and PCs, it is important to consider regional differences. An approach to ministry in the Northwest is very different from approaches to ministry in the Bible Belt of the Southeast. Therefore, it is important to consider more regional events.

6. The Effects of Short-term Pastoral Appointments

One of the primary weaknesses in the SBC21's ability to effect lasting change is pastoral length of stay. Short-term appointments undermine the process. How long a pastor stays in a church after receiving the training makes all the difference. Leadership is the key factor, both laity and clergy. So short-term appointments based on salary and tenure rather that fitness and gifts subverts SBC21.

Rev. Rasmus reports, "Our Baptist colleagues have been planting churches for the last 15 years. In many of those churches, seven years later the pastors that founded the churches are still pasturing—lives are being changed, people are coming in, things are happening."

One major problem for the SBC21 model is the appointment system of The United Methodist Church. Pastoral turnover both for CRCs and PCs has been a barrier to the long-term effectiveness of mentoring relationships and training events. Another problem is the appointment of pastors to churches who are a poor fit in terms of gifts and experience for where the congregation is in its development.

7. Learnings on What Does Not Work

PCs learn as much from what is not working as what is working in the CRCs. Rev. Rasmus has observed that, "What they (the PC) really needed to hear and see was what was really happening at St. John's. One day at conference one of the participants drifted off the conference scene and found himself behind the scenes where the people who did the day-to-day ministry were ministering. He found they weren't nearly as nice and accommodating as the conference leaders. Things were not running as smoothly as it appeared to be during the conference settings. He learned more during that short period than during all time spent in training."

Most CRCs teach only what is working, but avoid what is not working. It is important for the PC to know that the CRC does not have all the answers. It is equally important for the PC to know what does not work. Again Rev. Rasmus reflects, "The most important thing to share, especially with other pastors and laypersons as well, is what has caused me the biggest scars, created the biggest pain, and kept me up at night. They need to know what decisions caused me the greatest heartbreak."

8. The Value of One Big Idea

It is important that PCs leave with at least one big idea. This must be an intentional process to help PCs analyze what they have received from the CRC to determine what they can actually implement. The planning can begin at the training event itself.

The "Big Idea" is the innovation of St. John's. They felt it was important that PCs process the training that they received, while they were on site. This way they could go home with something that they were prepared to implement.

INSIGHTS GAINED

Joe Daniels of Emory, a congregation that went from a PC to CRC, shares his insights: "Strengthening the Black Church for the 21st Century is sorely needed in the Black Church in particular, but sorely needed in the broader Church as well. Our denomination is in serious decline. This is a major initiative to change that reality. This is one of the few general church initiatives focused upon changing that reality." Following are other insights from Rev. Daniels on SBC21.

1. Empowerment through Volunteer Peer Education

According to Rev. Daniels SBC21 is about empowerment. Empowerment comes through the realization that we all have the power to transform lives through knowledge we gain by following Christ in our daily ministry to the world. The initiative is unique because it transforms both lay and clergy of CRCs by helping them see that they, in spite of their weakness, have something to teach others. Likewise, PCs learn not from experts, but from people like themselves. This in turn empowers them to strive to be a teaching congregation by applying the knowledge they have received from their peers.

SBC21's true genius resides in its utilization of volunteer peer trainers versus paid staff or consultants. Knowledge and training from so-called experts is often disempowering because few are able to see themselves in their roles. Therefore, recipients of the training are often ambiguous about their ability to apply the lessons they have learned from experts. The fact that volunteers share their stories, experiences, and lessons learned out of love for the ministry and love of Christ rather than just their job, makes all the difference. Thus, rather than seeing themselves as clients or consumers of knowledge, persons from PCs truly become colleagues and collaborators in the work of the gospel.

2. The Spiritual Fervor of the Black Church

Rev. Daniels is convinced that the Black Church has a spiritual fervor about it for which the larger denomination needs and hungers. What SBC21 has enabled us to do on a broader scale is to tap into that fervor through worship, community/economic development, and congregation development in ways that can not only help Black congregations to grow, but also all congregations regardless of race, class, sexual preference, or ethnic origins. Therefore, the Black Church has the potential to be a powerful force for revival and revitalization of the whole church.

The spiritual fervor of the Black Church is one of the features that sets it apart from other churches, especially in The United Methodist Church. It is a fervor with roots not only in Africa, but also it is the fruit of the long suffering (brokenness) of African descendents on American soil. It has been watered by the blood of our ancestors and tears of generations uncounted, who cried out to God because of their afflictions. This spiritual fervor is now looked upon with awe and wonder because it possesses the passion of Christ's suffering on the cross. It likewise contains the joy of His resurrection.

3. Revived Churches as Catalysts

A revived church can act as a catalyst for the revitalization of a dying church. According to Rev. Daniels, "We have several examples of churches within our denomination that have turned around and have become revived literally from the ground up. Many of these churches are strong and are doing the kind of ministries that can serve as catalysts for the revival or revitalization of dying and declining churches." Emory UMC is one such church. It was nearly closed three times. Rudy and Juanita Rasmus' St. John's in Houston, (which was nearly closed itself) has been such a catalyst for Emory. Now Emory serves as a catalyst for Hughes Memorial UMC in Washington, D.C.

The SBC21 initiative provides the opportunity for churches to learn from these revived churches what it takes to become a strong church. For example, Emory focuses on issues of spiritual leadership, worship, community and economic development, discipleship, and congregational development. Each of these areas is critical for congregations to be strong within their community. Because of SBC21, there is a great opportunity for congregations to help other congregations to grow and develop regardless of race, class, and ethnic origins.

4. Annual Conference Support

The annual conference support can be the key to the success of SBC21. According to Rev. Daniels there were once three CRCs in the Baltimore-Washington annual conference: A.P Shaw UMC in Anacostia, John Wesley UMC in Baltimore, and Emory. Now there is only one in that conference. There needs to be more incentives for being a CRC and more emphasis placed on training events from the annual conference. The annual conference must take a more active role and have a greater voice. In addition to the support from annual conferences, SBC21 needs more support from resident bishops and their cabinets, who can in turn place it on the agenda of conference staff as well.

For SBC21 to be successful it has to avoid becoming ghettoized. It must become mainstreamed, as are other churchwide initiatives. The annual conference must promote it actively to congregations in need of revitalization. SBC21 is an excellent resource that is available for dying churches that are willing to grow; however, it is not talked about. One of the keys for SBC21 to reach its full potential is receiving more annual conference support.

5. Commitment to and Clarity of Calling

At the end of the day the question is this: Are pastors and congregations willing to give the energy it takes for revival and revitalization? It comes down to this: Do pastors or/and local congregations want to grow?

Jesus asked the lame man at the pool of Bethesda: Do you want to be made whole? (John 5:2-9) If pastors are not willing to invest the time, energy, blood, sweat, and tears to grow, all the efforts of SBC21 will be fruitless.

People have to be clear about what we are being called to do and become. There are pastors and congregations that are not clear about their calling. Ultimately revival and revitalization is the work of the Spirit. It requires dedication and commitment to the ministry of Jesus Christ. If one is not called to the work of the Spirit to raise dying churches to life, they will not be able to make the necessary sacrifices to see the work to its conclusion.

6. Jesus, The Disinvited

In Mark 5:1-17, we find the story of Jesus healing the Gerasene demoniac by permitting legions of demons to possess a herd of swine. This is a story of the redemptive love of God reclaiming a human life for community. This story illustrates that reclaiming human lives costs the community something. It costs more than they are willing to pay, so they disinvite Jesus from their neighborhood.

According to Rev. Daniels, this is what has happened in many of our United Methodist Churches. The reclaiming of the poor, the homeless, the addicted, the undocumented, and the incarcerated for our community may cost us too much in terms of our comfort level. Therefore, many have asked Jesus to leave their churches by our acts of inhospitality, unwillingness to change, and our lack of passion for the gospel.

Jesus has left many of our churches, as John Wesley feared, when Methodists no longer possessed fervor to serve the poor. Jesus has moved on to other communities of faith who welcome Jesus as in Matthew 25:31-46. The strength of the church comes from our ministry with the least of these. What we do with and for them, we do for Jesus. Not to be willing to pay the cost to reclaim human lives to community is to refuse the redemptive love of God and to disinvite Jesus from our communions.

7. Two Factors For Revival

There are two distinct factors that go into revival and revitalization of a church. These factors are anointed leadership and meeting the needs of the people. Anointed leaders are persons who are sure of their calling as leaders and have been filled with the Holy Spirit. They are filled with a passion for the work of the gospel. In other words, they have had their own

Aldersgate experience and have felt their hearts strangely warmed. According to Rev. Daniels, in scripture when revival or hope came into a community there were always leaders anointed by the Holy Ghost and equipped to lead God's people through transformation. Rev. Daniels claims, "In The United Methodist Church leadership appointments are often based on politics, promotion, and salary considerations. The question should always be do these leaders have the anointing to lead this community. Second, these leaders must be focused on meeting the needs of people both physical and spiritual. So they can meet the Christ that meets the needs."

Anointed leaders are agents of the redemptive love of God reclaiming human lives for community. Anointed leadership committed to meeting the needs of people requires a devotion to spiritual disciplines and rituals to sustain their spiritual fervor. Where you have anointed leaders committed to meeting needs, revival comes and churches are revitalized. When you have leaders who are appointed and not anointed, they often are committed to meeting their own needs and not the needs of the people. In these cases, death and stagnation comes. This is true not only in the Black Church but it transcends culture, class, and race.

IMPLICATIONS FOR THE FUTURE

Rev. Adrienne Terry is pastor of St. Matthews (an urban church), and former pastor of Franklin UMC (a rural church in southern Maryland). Both are PCs that participated in training events of SBC21 over the life of the initiative. Rev. Terry shares the implication of SBC21: "I love the Strengthening the Black Church training model. I believe it is an effective training model. I am sure that the general church can learn a great deal from the models that are designed around the specific topics SBC21 comes up with. They can learn a lot from resources that are provided during the training and in terms of how to put together a relevant training event. I think that the general church can learn a lot from the trainers. I am convinced that God allowed this initiative to happen in this way to celebrate the strength in the Black Church."

In the pages that follow, Rev. Terry evaluates the implications for PCs, CRCs, and the general church.

IMPLICATIONS FOR PARTNER CONGREGATIONS

1. A Community for Minority Congregations

SBC21 creates community for minority congregations who feel isolated within a majority denomination. Rev. Terry has had extensive experience with SBC21 as a pastor of two congregations that became PCs. The first was Franklin UMC, a 150-year-old congregation with attendance on Sunday of about 80 to 100, with approximately 250 members on the roll. They attended a three-day training event on congregational development held at Ben Hill UMC in Atlanta, Georgia. This congregation had not participated in training events at the conference or district levels. Therefore, one of Rev. Terry's goals was to broaden their training experience so they could interact with other congregations who were like them. One of the major problems with Black United Methodist Churches is often the feeling of isolation within a largely White denomination. A SBC21 training event creates a community of like congregations with similar backgrounds and struggles. Even the act of leaving their community was new and a good thing for this congregation. Because they had been an insulated congregation, one implication of the training was the creation of community to address the issue of isolation.

2. The SBC21 Application Process

Part of the challenge in participating in the SBC21 event was completing the application. (See application in Appendix E.) It involved the leadership writing down their goals and expectations, which was something that the congregation had not done before. This process required the leadership to enter into a period of self-reflection and self-assessment to which they were not accustomed. As a result, the critical assessment of their congregational practices of ministry and calling, led them to ponder previously unquestioned activities and ways of thinking. This had implications on how they perceived the training and its potential impact on the congregation.

3. Financial Resources and Participation

The best part was the financial resources that allowed the congregation to participate in experiences they would have never been able to do on their own. Rev. Terry's second PC, St. Matthews, average Sunday morning attendance is between 65 to 90 with about 200 members on the roll. According to Rev. Terry it is an urban church with rural roots. They attended an event in South Carolina called "Let Us Worship." During the event they attended worship services and workshops over a three-day weekend at three different churches. Rev. Terry stated, "It was a great experience that we could not have participated in if it were not for the financial resources provided by SBC21."

4. The Benefit of New Opportunities

The strength of training was getting participants out of their comfort zone. To geographically remove them out of their neighborhood to an unfamiliar setting was important to expanding their horizons as to what is possible. Many small churches are so insulated that they become stagnated, frozen in the past, and new ideas are difficult to penetrate their comfort zones. New venues offer opportunities for some vulnerability to the novel and the new.

5. An Increase in Worship Participation

Persons involved in SBC21 training experienced an increased confidence level. One of the primary observable results for those who attended the events was a marked increase in confidence as worship leaders and participants. By exposing participants to other congregational leaders like themselves, moving them out of their comfort zones, and providing training in cutting edge worship practices, the church leaders developed a new level of confidence. This newfound confidence is evident by increased participation in worship.

IMPLICATIONS FOR CONGREGATIONAL RESOURCE CENTERS

1. The Importance of On-site Planning

If one of the goals of SBC21 training was to have PCs replicate the training event at their own church or community, it would have been helpful to begin that planning process while on site. In the future, it will be important that training events include planning for postevent activities. By doing so, the resources and trainers are available to answer questions and PC leadership are still in a teachable moment. St. Matthews went to training with intention to plan the same kind of event for their congregation, but ultimately they really could not do it.

2. The Need for Implementation Follow-up

If PCs are expected to share their experience and engage in post training activities, then targeted long-term follow-up is needed for them to be effective. According to Rev. Terry, someone from SBC21 staff called immediately afterward about the event itself and months later they called again. We gave them feedback by phone and written comments concerning the event and its effectiveness. "I think they met their goals but they did not meet our goals." The SBC21 has done a good job documenting the model and follow-up to determine its quality and effectiveness of the CRC and the training events. However, what is needed is follow-up to help PCs implement what they have learned.

3. A Lack of Innovation

Rev. Terry said she has not enrolled in any training for the last two years because the initiative itself has lost some of its freshness through a lack of innovation. If the initiative is going to continue to serve the church for the long run, it will have to continue to grow and be transformed. "What I see going on now is a cycle of training SBC21 that is pretty much the same. It appears that they have gotten into a rut of doing the same things over and over again. I think they have found something that worked and have gotten into their own comfort zone," stated Rev. Terry.

4. Generalized Versus Specialized Training

SBC21 will need to pay more careful attention to the congregation's internal resources before the training in order to design sessions that will have the desired impact of revitalization and revival. If not, SBC21 runs the risk of developing generalized events that do not meet the needs of specific congregations.

Even though one of the strengths of SBC21 is its preevent application process, it would take more surveys to assess each congregation's specific needs and potentials. Otherwise, the training's focus is for a general audience. Rev. Terry says, "What attracted me in the first place to SBC21 was how intentional and specific the training was designed around specific needs of the congregations being trained. This is why, I felt, I could respond to the invitation by taking a group to be trained. More intentional surveys to ascertain who the audiences are that are going to be trained is important."

IMPLICATION FOR THE GENERAL CHURCH

1. Benefits for the General Church

The general church can benefit from SBC21's comprehensive training framework. Especially beneficial is the preevent planning and application process. Rev Terry comments, "The preparticipation forms that they sent out are very helpful. I think those trainings are very good. They need some work, but they are better than what I have seen in the general church. The SBC21 training events really pulled on really strong trainers. I don't think they made the assumption that if you are a really good pastor, then you are therefore a good trainer. The training framework that identified the host pastor and host congregation is very important. Also the material that was used was culturally relevant. They spent a lot of time pouring over relevant material."

2. SBC21 Products

Rev. Terry believes SBC21 needs to become technologically savvy. She states, "I think we need to explore the development of products at the next stage. There needs to be books, tapes, curriculum, DVD, etc. If I were a funder, I would want to see more tangible products. We need more techno savvy. We need to reach this new generation."

Rev. Terry reflects, "My daughter is in her thirties and what she thinks is relevant training is different from what I think is relevant. She would rather watch a training event on the computer. They don't need to call me because they can text message me." SBC21 needs to come out with a DVD series. A Trainer-of-Trainer model that will allow people to go back to their church and use the DVD package.

ANALYSIS

All three pastors agree that SBC21 training is a good model that the Black Church needs in particular and The United Methodist Church needs in general. They are enthusiastic about their participation and believe their respective congregation benefited greatly whether as a CRC or PC. Yet, they are willing to admit that all congregations did not or would not benefit due to the lack of readiness or willingness to grow and be revitalized. Many PCs waste their time and the SBC21 initiative money. While our informants view the preparticipation process as a strong aspect of the model, they all agree it needs to be strengthened. Selecting PCs that are ready to grow and matching them with the proper CRC is critical to the model.

There was also agreement that the SBC21 cannot stand alone. It must have the support and cooperation of the resident bishop, cabinet, and conference staff of the annual conference in several ways. First, the appointment system must allow pastoral leadership to remain in place long enough for the SBC21 training to take hold. Leaders should be appointed based on the needs of the congregation and abilities of the leaders without regards to any other considerations. Second, the annual conference needs to actively promote the SBC21 initiative. Incentives should be provided to encourage churches to participate either as a CRC or PC. Third, SBC21 should be on the agenda of conference staff in order that it may be viewed as a useful tool to address the needs of distressed congregation.

The SBC21 model must continue evolving in order to assure that its training meets the specific needs of PCs. It should avoid becoming a one-size-fits-all training model. All SBC21 training should adopt the "Big Idea" practice initiated by St. John's, which allows the PC to begin action planning while on the CRC site. In addition to the standard follow-up evaluation, follow-up should also be performed to help implement what the PCs learned during the training.

Yet, the underlying finding in our study is that vitality cannot be divorced from clarity of mission and certainty of the message. The bottom line is leaders, whether clergy or lay, and congregations must be clear about their call. No amount of training can substitute for a heart to serve the poor and willingness to be reconciled to God and neighbor.

Robert M. Franklin, in his call to action, *Crisis in the Village: Restoring Hope in African American Communities*, states boldly and clearly: *The black community needs African American Methodists, all of them, to step up and take responsibility for leading the educational renewal of the entire village.*[3] Franklin estimates that there are twenty thousand Black Methodist churches with over 8 million members in the three major Black Methodist traditions (The African Methodist Episcopal, African American Episcopal Zion, and The Christian Methodist Episcopal Churches) combined with African Americans in The United Methodist Church.[4] One can only imagine what it would mean to the African American Village in Crisis if SBC21 were to expand to include the Pan-Methodist. African American Methodists in vital congregations with a clear call to restore the village can be a powerful force for reclaiming human lives for community. However, reconciling the broken covenant of the Methodist communion is just as important. For Franklin the crisis in the Black Church is not one of vitality but of mission. In final analysis, strengthening the Black Church is a process of creating shared mission between the CRCs and the PCs. Rev. Rasmus and Rev. Daniels assert that PCs that affirm their mission to the poor are congregations that do what it takes to become vital congregations.

III. THE MESSAGE: BE RECONCILED TO GOD!

All this is from God, who reconciled us to himself through Christ, and has given us the ministry of reconciliation; that is in Christ God was reconciling the world to himself, not counting their trespasses against them, and entrusting the message of reconciliation to us. So we are ambassadors for Christ, since God is making his appeal through us; we entreat you on behalf of Christ, be reconciled to God.

(2 Corinthians 5:18-20)

Finally, to strengthen the Black Church for the twenty-first century is about more than a model or even the mission; it ultimately is about a message. This message is the reason why the church came into being. This message is the reason that the church is made strong. Ultimately, this message is the reason God gave his only begotten Son so that we might be saved.

The Methodist Church from its inception has witnessed and participated in the struggles of Black people throughout history and all over the world. John Wesley viciously attacked the slave trade. Richard Allen, Absalom Jones, and James Varick left the Methodist Episcopal Church after the insults of broken covenant. The Methodist Episcopal Church was split North and South over the question of slavery. After reuniting, it was split again with the creation of the Central Conference that segregated Black Methodist congregants from their White brothers and sisters. Through all this, the Black Church within The United Methodist Church remained steadfast. This is the evidence of the dogged strength of the Black Church in The United Methodist Church and its predecessor bodies.

When we have broken covenant with Christ by breaking covenant with each other, we are all broken people regardless of our race or ethnic origin. A reading of the documents presented to the 1996 General Conference makes it clear that the Strengthening the Black Church for the 21st Century Initiative was an effort to redress the benign neglect of over 200 years by broken ecclesia structures. Yet, from the beginning, the Black Methodist Church thought not of itself, but of the whole body of Methodism as it always has. This is the gift of wholeness that the Black Church within United Methodism brings to the brokenness of Methodism. This fracture is largely due to the curse of White racism. The true strength of the Black Methodist Church is the message *"be reconciled to God."*

The Black Church, by making central it's hope in Christ and not in human structures, has held on to the redemptive love of God. The CRCs are strong because they spend their vitality reclaiming broken human lives for community as evidenced by Adrienne Terry of St. Matthews, Rudy and Juanita Rasmus of St. John's and Joseph Daniels of Emory. Likewise the lesson to be learned by SBC21 for the whole Methodist body of believers is that we must become Ambassadors of Christ, reclaiming human lives for community. If we continue to focus on saving dying churches, we lose our souls.

Our efforts at saving dying churches is a vain attempt to save face, pride at not wanting to admit failure. Instead, we should focus on new life in the gospel by seeking to spread the message of Christ to a materialistic and hedonistic world in need of spiritual revival. If we let the dead bury the dead and follow Christ by giving up our vanity for the message, our churches will experience revival and revitalization.

Finally, to follow Jesus Christ is to heed his call to unity in the Beloved Community. This again is the gift of the Black Church, which with its mere presence after centuries of insult, neglect, and outright rejection remains, while others have left to form their own denominations. While many take this as a sign of weakness, it has proven to be evidence of great strength. The Strengthening the Black Church for the 21st Century Initiative offers the Church a Mission, a Model, and a Message—Be Reconciled to God!

A SUMMARY

Broken covenant and broken people are not powerful enough to prevent the redemptive love of God from reclaiming human lives for community. It, therefore, is by and through Jesus Christ, that we are called to the unity of the beloved community.

(1996 General Conference, General and Judicial Administration)

NOTES

1. W.E.B. Dubois, *The Soul of Black Folks*, with an Introduction by Henry Louis Gates, Jr. (New York: Bantam Books, 1989), 3.
2. "The Story of Songs of Zion: Pioneering Paths in a Strange Land," paper written by the Rev. William B. McClain, 2005.
3. Robert M. Franklin, *Crisis in the Village* (Minneapolis: Fortress Press, 2007), 144–145.
4. Ibid., 144.

CHAPTER SEVEN

STANDING ON THE PROMISES: LOOKING TO THE FUTURE

THE HOPE OF SBC21

Bishop Jonathan D. Keaton

Deliverance from the slings and arrows of racism remains a prevailing hope for Black folk in the church. The United Methodist Church is no exception. That is why the words and promises of Jesus are so important. To hear in Luke 4:17-19 that Christ comes "to preach good news to the poor . . . to set at liberty the oppressed"(RSV) is assurance that God will not abandon those in bondage. Christ is the Good Shepherd bringing "life and that abundantly" to the people of God (John 10:10). Because no aspect of African American life in the church can sequester itself from the effects of racism and/or its children, this is especially good news. At the same time, Black Methodists long for an equal opportunity to share their gifts and graces with The United Methodist Church, to share in its responsibilities, to experience true acceptance, and to have their ministry needs addressed.

Occasionally, the church manages to catch the spirit of such expectations and create a vital ministry to address those needs in some fashion.

One such vital ministry is SBC21. For a number of participants, SBC21 is bringing a measure of hope and help to African American clergy and laity who want to grow their churches spiritually and numerically.

For example, in a 2004 video produced by SBC21 for the whole church, a golden-ager made this statement about her young pastor, "He is not a four-wall pastor. He gets out into the community." Roderick Martin, recent convert at the South Columbus UMC, described himself as "a lost little boy whom everyone gave up on." Not so with South Columbus UMC, they invited Roderick and his football gang to join them in ministry. Roderick joined the church and is now a lay leader in the church. The Rev. Dr. Lillie Madison Jones, Ministries Team Coordinator for the Western North Carolina Conference attended two SBC21 training events in Huger, South Carolina and South Columbus UMC in Georgia. These powerful and transformative events led Dr. Jones to three conclusions: (1) the pride and history of the Black Church is being operationalized; (2) where understanding money management is a transforming agent (when done in accordance to God's principles), it leads to paying of apportionments; and (3) proper training for youth and young adults can lead to them becoming future leaders. These stories and testimonies are just one aspect of the programmatic hopes fulfilled by SBC21.

When participants learn that SBC21 has support at the highest level of the church, that is, General Conference, belief increases that things may be different. Such support generates the hope that change is on the way and that the whole church values the gifts of the Black Church. Add to this awareness, the fact that SBC21 provides financial support for a team of five (the pastor and four laity) to attend a training event sponsored by a CRC. The sense that the whole church cares about issues important to the Black Church is confirmed.

Yet, the sense of thanksgiving is always tempered by the haunting history of the past, the present, and the likely future. However Black folk "live, move, and have their being," The United Methodist Church has always struggled with their presence. Questions like the following are heard often: How much more do they need? How long is it necessary to carry on these special programs? Can't we just program together? Aren't we better together? Questions like these about SBC21 or any other ministry focused on the Black Church have usually been posed for more than informational reasons. Time and again, church history has demonstrated that the shelf life for such emphases is relatively short and contentious. For instance, the church's stance on slavery was overturned almost as quickly as it is affirmed.

Division meant more than unity in 1844; owning slaves was the powder keg. Division meant more than church unity in 1939; the Central Jurisdiction was created. At the 2000 General Conference in Cleveland, Ohio, the church emphasized reconciliation and repentance for "those who left" over those "those who stayed."

That said, three General Conferences adopted a committee that has greatly enhanced the work and success of SBC21. General Conference created a Coordinating Committee charged with the responsibility of overseeing and implementing the Plan of Action. This included hiring staff coordinators, attending to budgetary and fiscal matters, selecting CRCs, establishing guidelines and criteria for CRCs and the Partner Congregations, interpretating and promoting findings throughout The United Methodist Church.

Hence, SBC21 does not compete for time and attention alongside other important matters in the portfolio of responsibilities carried by general agency staff. Secondly, the twenty-three members on the committee, clergy and laity, are members of the Black Church. In short, they have a stake in its present and future. So does the leadership of the whole church. For instance, representatives from the five jurisdictions are nominees of the five Colleges of Bishops in the United States. Two persons are the selections of National BMCR. By the decision of the Council of Bishops, two youth, two young adults, and two bishops participate in SBC21. Third, each general agency and commission names one person to resource the committee. These persons are and have been invaluable to the work of SBC21. With their commitment and knowledge, SBC21 has made even greater progress.

Last, but not least CRCs, lead the way. Transformation and inspiration is occurring across the church in rural, urban, and suburban congregations. Training opportunities and follow up provided by the CRCs to PC are making a positive difference. In no way am I implying that everything SBC21 touches automatically becomes a Windsor Village in Houston, a St. Luke Community in Dallas or a Saint Mark in Wichita, Kansas. But the PCs that learn the lessons of the trainings, and adapt them for their situations constantly report that the life and ministry of their church is indeed strengthened.

And What of the Future?

When this bishop ruminates over ten years of the SBC21 story, hears and witnesses SBC21 delivering all kinds of local churches to new life and possibility, it makes real the name of Emmanuel (God is with us). Yet SBC21 can never be the full essence of God's will for the whole church.

In a sentence, SBC21 is the latest stance taken by The United Methodist Church and its predecessor bodies on behalf of Black folk.

Whenever General Conference chooses to exercise its option with regard to SBC21, the issues of race, equal opportunity, acceptance of Black folk and the particular needs of the Black Church will remain. The prevailing question will rise again for the church to answer. New generations of the Black Church will raise it. How are we delivered from the slings and arrows of racism in the church? It is common knowledge that National BMCR have successfully advocated for the creation of the General Commission on Religion and Race, the Black Staff Forum, Black Community Developers, the Black College Fund, the Ethnic Minority Local Church, the election of Ebony Bishops, General Secretaries, general agency staff, and SBC21. The abundant life, which Christ offers, is all around us, usually brought to life when the slings and arrows of racism become so overbearing that BMCR can do no other. More than that, we serve a God continually making all things new. New revelations emerge as times change. Since National BMCR has been the progenitor of new emphases relative to the souls of Black folk; it is likely that BMCR or its child will stand in the gap and call the church to continued faithfulness to those of us "who stayed" unless by happenstance Black Methodism dies or is once more separated from the fold analogous to The Christian Methodist Episcopal Church. From my view, that fate is highly unlikely. From its inception, Black Methodists have been a part of the Methodist Church. I believe that Black presence will continue in The United Methodist Church till the end of time. That is our heritage. And that is our legacy.

HOPE AND HISTORY RHYME

Bishop Peter D. Weaver

"And hope and history rhyme" is a refrain woven through Seamus Heaney's epic poem "The Cure of Troy" which was inspired by Nelson Mandela's return from prison.[1] In the over two hundred year epic history of African Americans and the Methodist movement in America, SBC21 is one of God's moments when hope and history have rhymed. The results are new strength not only for the Black Church but also for the whole church in its effective witness and mission for Jesus Christ in this new century.

When Harry Hosier and Francis Asbury rode together and drew on each other's strengths at the beginning of our movement, the witness for Christ was stronger, the reach of evangelism wider, the embrace of the variety of gifts broader, and the prophetic word of inclusion more clearly lived than at any time in our history. The acculturation of the Methodist movement and the sin of racism might well have destroyed the early promise of Methodism. But faithful African Americans believed that inspite of oppression and injustice, the strength of the Black Church could not be denied. As the SBC21 report to the 1996 General Conference affirmed, "broken covenant and broken people are not powerful enough to prevent the redemptive love of God from reclaiming human lives."[2]

The 1996 General Conference, held in Denver, Colorado, celebrated the strengths of the approximately 2,500 predominantly Black United Methodist Churches. At the same time it noted a 32 percent decline in the number of Black United Methodist Churches in the United States and a 15 percent decline in Black membership from 1974 to 1992. The General Council of Ministries, responding to the report of a 1992–96 study chaired by Bishop Woodie W. White, proposed to the General Conference SBC21 "as a gift, not just to the Black Church, but to the whole church—a gift filled with hope and possibilities for transformation. Vital congregations within the Black community will lead the way!"[3]

Leading the Way

As a gift to the whole church, SBC21 has led the way in the implementation of four innovative strategies for the transformation of congregations: Clear Definition of Vital Congregation, Congregation Based, Clergy/Laity Teaming, and Comprehensive Strength for the Future. These are critical for looking to the future.

1. Clear Definition of Vital Congregation

After much study, clear characteristics of vital congregations were identified. Too often in the past "vitality" was a vague subjective description reflective of large numbers more than anything else. Six primary characteristics based on theological integrity and empirical evidence were offered by SBC21. These could be summarized as: 1) Effective leadership (lay and clergy) "informed, educated, creative, energetic, biblically and theologically grounded" 2) "takes seriously the full range of developmental, spiritual, social and material needs" of all persons... "passionate and compassionate" 3) vital "worship, singing, devotion, prayer, praise, and preaching in varied traditions" 4) "Bible study in small groups" for "life in contemporary situations" 5) "Effective planning and administration… comprehensive and broad-based" 6) "deep streams of spirituality" and "acts on needs… social-political, cultural, and economic… church, community, nation, world."[4]

This clarity of definition, which continued to evolve, gave SBC21 important means for evaluation and focused outcomes as the program developed.

2. Congregation Based

The second important principal of SBC21 was that the focus and resourcing were all congregation based. Real, living congregations were the resource for teaching and learning. Congregations were partnered with congregations. Covenant, coaching relationships were developed between congregations. The process was not just thinking about theory in some distant seminar classroom, but experiencing the practice of ministry in real churches with real roofs to be repaired, in real communities with challenging problems, and with less than perfect laity and pastors.

Initially, the goal was to establish twenty-five congregations as resource centers to provide training and partnership with 400–600 teams of laity and clergy. The resourcing congregations were of all sizes and geographical locations. All of the churches become both learners and teachers.

3. Clergy/Laity Teaming

SBC21 from the beginning required that congregations seeking to become stronger must have laity and clergy on the teams coming for resourcing. Likewise, those providing the resourcing needed to be both clergy and laity. The clergy could not "go it alone."

Historically, the United Methodist movement has been the most effective when laity and clergy "teamed" their various gifts and perspectives in serving Christ and the community. It is also our future. Extraordinary gifts of time and talent are abundantly available with the growing number of retirees in many communities. Young people are eager to participate in congregations that welcome their gifts, fresh perspectives, and hands-on involvement.

Further, the development of lay leadership is critical to the continuity of vitality and strength in a congregation when there is pastoral transition. SBC21 has taken the long view in seeking to assure strength in our churches that stands on the foundation of the whole congregation, not just the pastor.

4. Comprehensive Strength for the Future

It was quickly evident that SBC21 was strengthening the whole United Methodist movement. Many of the Black churches had been born out of congregations that had evolved from one primary racial/ethnic characteristic to another as communities around them made transitions. Now many predominantly Black churches are changing as the populations around them are in transition. In the earliest programs by SBC21, laity and pastors from all kinds of transitional communities were coming for resourcing. The whole church was learning the importance of diversity centered in Christ.

With the increasingly rich diversity in America now and in the future more of our congregations will benefit from SBC21 resources. Ultimately, the goal of SBC21 has never been to strengthen the status quo. But like Harry Hosier and Francis Asbury, who rode together for the sake of what Christ could bring to this new world that was developing before their very eyes, so we move forward enriched by all the strengths in our movement.

The twenty-first century is such a time for us. Ministry that is comprehensive in its strength and embrace will continue to emerge out of congregations with laity and clergy teams that are clear about the definition of strong, vital ministry and seek to make disciples of Jesus Christ for the transformation of the world. SBC21 has helped all of us to see in fresh ways how "hope and history" can rhyme. It has prepared us for the new future God is giving The United Methodist Church.

STRETCHING TOWARDS THE VISION

Bishop James King

Not long ago I was entering the nursing home to visit my mother. Standing in the reception area was one of the residents. I had seen this man on several occasions. It was a common experience to share friendly smiles toward one another but then I noticed he was standing over a 300-piece picture puzzle that was partially completed. As I exited the nursing home the man was still standing near the puzzle. I commented on the challenge before him and he responded in the affirmative as he pointed to another puzzle box that someone had given him saying: "Yes and there is another one that was given to me. It has 500 pieces, and when you finish with it, it glows!"

As I departed from the presence of this resident our conversation stayed with me. I thought later on that the vision God has for God's kingdom to come on earth as it is in heaven leaves us with a beautiful picture of all creation. Like a picture puzzle that includes many pieces, the church has parts—pieces if you will—that are fragile, damaged and broken that must be restored before the church is whole and functioning as it should. However, when the church as the body of Christ begins to operate efficiently as God's redemptive instrument for Kingdom building, it glows.

SBC21 was established in 1996 by the General Conference "to develop an avenue by which United Methodist churches with predominantly Black congregations would become effective in mission and ministry." SBC21 has been identifying Black Churches that are glowing and partnering them with those congregations that no longer have a glowing vision. The United Methodist Church understands well the need to give special attention to many segments of the church as we stretch towards the vision of God's Kingdom to manifest itself among us. SBC21 reflects by its mere existence the fact that the Black Church is a crucial piece of the puzzle that must receive appropriate attention if it is to find its rightful place in the picture of God's vision. So SBC21 continues to stretch toward a vision that is based on God's promise through God's holy word. Paul reminds us in Romans 4:21-22 of the importance of faith in response to God's promise: "No distrust made him waiver concerning the promise of God, but he grew stronger in his faith as he gave glory to God, being fully convinced that God was able to do what he had promised."

Positive Persistence Pays

As with Abraham and Sarah, the journey that leads into the mission that is carved out for us by God can be a long and tedious one. SBC21 has been created for unique and special mission within The United Methodist Church. The bottom line is that SBC21 is to help make the Black Church stronger. This significant piece of the puzzle needs restoration in order that the entire mosaic may witness signs of God' reign in the world through the church.

The core strategy employed to help strengthen the Black Church has been CRCs. I would point out that the nobler the task the more one has to be persistent. It will take time to accomplish the goal that fulfills the purpose of SBC21. It took time for Noah to build the ark. It took time for Moses to lead the Hebrews to the Promise Land. Much time in prayer and praise preceded the disciples' experience of the promise of a divine Holy Spirit-filled moment. It will take time for SBC21 to complete its mission.

Regarding Abraham the Bible states: "No distrust made him waiver concerning the promise of God." The great temptation that accompanies any mission from God is to quit too soon. Once you go on the battlefield for God, it is not yours to win. It is God's. The road to any promise land is hard and difficult. There is often much resistance. The walls of Jericho are stubborn. Just as Abraham did not waiver, nor must the church. If this is of God, we must press on to finding increasing ways to support what God has promised. Though difficult, the work that belongs to SBC21 is essential and possible to achieve. We must not quit. In the song "I Don't Feel No Ways Tired," James Cleveland states, "I don't believe He brought me this far to leave me." It is a long and tedious journey, but God cannot fail. When God says it, the question is not if it will happen but when it will happen. The vision that God gives and promises to fulfill shall come to past. Sometimes voices in the middle of the wilderness journey will cry out "turn back we are not getting any where," but do not waiver, Church. With a positive attitude, look towards the vision and keep your feet firmly planted on the promises of God.

Doubt and despair are enemies of success. They can have a toxic effect on any plan that is built on hope. Faith on the other hand does not need evidence to go forward. Faith alone provides the necessary fuel to press towards the mark, no matter how difficult the mission. I have seen congregations that have caused me to pause and wonder in my flesh, but when I realize it is not my promise nor my mission but God's, I see the possibilities and become more determined.

I am aware of numerous congregations that point to SBC21 with thanksgiving for helping them to experience new life and vitality as they learned from partner congregations. Many congregations have been blessed because SBC21 has continued to exist and did not waiver. If one believes in God and God makes a promise, then you may need to rest for a while but do not stop until the promise has been fulfilled. God is greater than any opposition. SBC21 is a step in the right direction and must continue to move forward with all the support the General Church can provide.

Celebrate the Victories

It has been my experience in the church that far too often we do not celebrate enough of what the Lord has done. It appears as if someone or something slapped the hand of pastors and congregations because they confused boasting about what they had accomplished versus what God has done. Boasting on the Lord's work is always in order and appropriate. The more you boast on what God has done, the stronger you become in believing that God will do even more. Psalms 68:32-35 (*The New Interpreter's Study Bible*) tells us:

> Sing to God, O kingdoms of the earth;
>   sing praises to the Lord, ...
> Ascribe power to God,
>   whose majesty is over Israel;
>   and whose power is in the skies.
> Awesome is God in his sanctuary,
>   the God of Israel;
> he gives power and strength to his people.
> Blessed be God!

When you want something to live, give it attention. Conversely, if you want something to grow weaker, give it little or no attention at all. Abraham "grew strong in his faith as he gave glory to God." Isn't that amazing! God gets the glory and you get stronger. Is this not the witness of Peter who got stronger the more he focused on Jesus? Is this not the witness of David who appeared fearless against the giant Goliath? And what about Esther who was encouraged to focus on what God could be doing through her life?

As we give glory and praise to God for SBC21 as it enables more and more churches to experience vitality as well as more involvement of bishops, cabinets, conferences, and districts, we focus on the good things being done. Just as Abraham's faith grew as he addressed the daunting task before him, so will faith in SBC21 continue to gain momentum. The more attention we focus on God and the power of God's promise, and the less we focus on ourselves and all the things we cannot do and the lack of resources, the less likely we are to grow weary and consider giving up prematurely.

God Can Do Anything But Fail

Our God is an awesome God! If we believe this truth then we are prepared to ask the same question that Sara received. "Is there anything too hard for God?" It is easy to become timid and shy as we travel along life's highway. We are often disappointed in the flesh by broken promises, scarred by misplaced trust, and hurt by people and institutions. It is easy to become cynical, expecting little and prepared for less. Paul reminds us that we are to be like Abraham who was fully convinced that God was able to do what he had promised. Once we are convinced, once we put our trust in God, passion and determination rise up in us and nothing is impossible for us because we realize we are standing on the promises of God.

Every time I hear the Mississippi Mass Choir sing "God Is Able" I am inspired and encouraged to keep pressing on. Unfortunately the path to the promise land is not always straight but includes curves and barriers along the way. Moses and the Hebrews had to make numerous adjustments. Samuel had to wait upon the last son in Jesse's house before God was pleased. David was anointed to be King of Israel but it would take time before what God had promised materialized. God has chosen the church as an instrument of redemption. However, a church that begins on a weak foundation or loses sight of the vision over the years can produce strong arguments for maintaining the status quo even when some of the leadership is ready to move forward. Thus, being convinced to stand on the promises of God we must keep our eyes on the vision while making appropriate adjustments.

SBC21 has an accountability component built into operational guidelines.

It is important that SBC21 continues to monitor every aspect of its purpose with a commitment to hold to its values. SBC21 has some outstanding and committed leaders on the Coordinating Committee. Through efficient measurement systems that hold each vital link of the strategy together, hopefully it will continue to evaluate objectively and adjust as necessary. All the parts must interact around one goal and one goal only... and that is a stronger more vital congregations.

In the cartoon Ziggy, a car has come to a stop near a sign that reads "Road to Happiness." Beyond the sign you can see a beautiful skyline leading to a breathtaking sunset, and a meandering road leading around a hillside where one could easily imagine some form of utopia on the other side of the mountain. But the reason the car has come to a halt is because there is another sign that has been attached to the first sign and it reads "Road under construction." Beautiful People, we are the construction workers to a Christ like world. We are the ones to put the puzzle together to that road that leads to God's Kingdom on earth as it is in heaven. Let us continue to stretch towards that day when all God's people are at the table, filled with value and joy because all have been nurtured into wholeness. Therefore, we are still stretching towards the vision as we stand on the promises of God!

NOTES

1. Kader Asmal, David Chedesta, and Wilmot James, eds., *Nelson Mandela: In His Own Words.* (London: Little Brown, 2003), xx.
2. *Daily Christian Advocate:* Advance ed., 1, (1996) General Conference, 580.
3. Ibid., 580.
4. Ibid., 587.

APPENDICES

Note: If you are interested in obtaining a listing of SBC21 partner churches or a directory of African American United Methodist Churches, please contact the SBC21 office: phone - (615)320-1722; email - pholman@ gbod.org. Also available is an *Annotated Bibliography of Acricentric Resources* compiled by Mary Love and published by the National Council of the Churches of Christ in the USA and Hood Theological Seminary. Order by phone at 212-870-2151.

Appendix A: Our United Methodist Family Tree

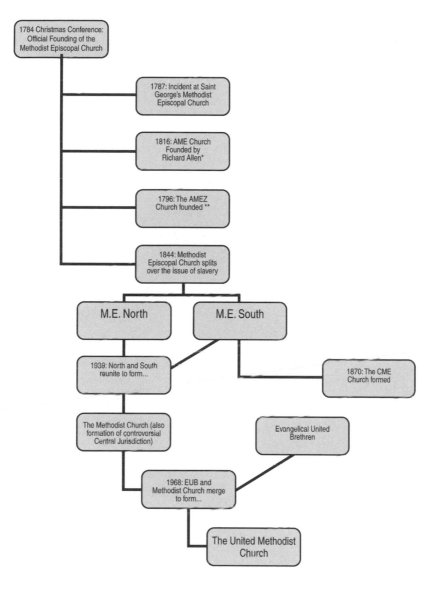

1784 Christmas Conference: Official Founding of the Methodist Episcopal Church

1787: Incident at Saint George's Methodist Episcopal Church

1816: AME Church Founded by Richard Allen*

1796: The AMEZ Church founded **

1844: Methodist Episcopal Church splits over the issue of slavery

M.E. North

M.E. South

1939: North and South reunite to form...

1870: The CME Church formed

The Methodist Church (also formation of controversial Central Jurisdiction)

Evangelical United Brethren

1968: EUB and Methodist Church merge to form...

The United Methodist Church

* Some sources cite 1815, (See chapter 1, note 53)

** See chapter 1, note 55 for other dates connected to the AMEZ church founding

APPENDIX B: DIRECTORY BY QUADRENNIUM

2005–2008 QUADRENNIUM
COORDINATING COMMITTEE MEMBERS

Episcopal Representation

Bishop Jonathan D. Keaton, Chair	North Central Jurisdiction	Michigan Area
Bishop James R. King	Southeastern Jurisdiction	Louisville Area

North Central Jurisdiction — **Annual Conference**

Dr. Carolyn Johnson, Vice Chair — North Indiana Annual Conference
Rev. Benita Rollins — East Ohio Annual Conference
Mr. Carnell Scott — North Indiana Annual Conference

Northeast Jurisdiction

Mr. Ernest Swiggett, Finance Chair — New York Annual Conference
Rev. Dr. Dorothy Watson Tatem, Evaluation Chair — Eastern Pennsylvania Annual Conference
Mrs. Darlene Webb — Peninsula-Delaware Annual Conference

South Central Jurisdiction

Ms. Deborah Bell, Program Co-Chair — Arkansas Annual Conference
Rev. Tyrone Gordon, Program Chair — North Texas Annual Conference
Rev. Jackye Waiters-Lee, Secretary — North Texas Annual Conference

Southeastern Jurisdiction

Mrs. Rubielee Addison — South Carolina Annual Conference
Mr. Curtis Henderson — Alabama/West Florida Annual Conference
Rev. Joseph Roberson — South Georgia Annual Conference

Western Jurisdiction

Rev. LLC Hammond, Finance Vice-Chair — California-Pacific Annual Conference
Mr. Bobby McCray — Desert Southwest Annual Conference
Rev. James McCray — California-Nevada Annual Conference

BMCR Representatives

Bishop Melvin Talbert	Executive Director, BMCR
Rev. Joseph Crawford (2007)	North Indiana Conference
Rev. Vincent Harris (2005)	Texas Annual Conference
Mr. James Salley (2006)	Tennessee Annual Conference

Youth Representatives

Ms. Ashley Jasper	East Ohio Annual Conference
Mr. Nelson-Mandela Nance	North Texas Annual Conference

Young Adult Representatives

Dr. Larry Hygh, Communication Chair	California-Pacific Annual Conference
Mr. Henry Stewart	Baltimore-Washington Annual Conference

SBC21 Staff

Mrs. Cheryl Stevenson, National Coordinator	Kansas West Annual Conference
Ms. Felicia Hampton, Assistant to National Coordinator (2005)	
Ms. Pam Holman, Assistant to National Coordinator (2006)	
Dr. Linda Crowell, Follow Up Consultant	East Ohio Annual Conference

2001–2004 QUARDRENNIUM
COORDINATING COMMITTEE MEMBERS

Episcopal Representation

Bishop Jonathan D. Keaton, Chair	North Central Jurisdiction	East Ohio Area
Bishop Peter D. Weaver	Northeast Jurisdiction	Philadelphia Area

North Central Jurisdiction — **Annual Conference**

Mr. Paul Hobson — Northern Illinois Annual Conference
Dr. Carolyn Johnson, Vice Chair — North Indiana Annual Conference
Rev. Benita Rollins — East Ohio Annual Conference

Northeastern Jurisdiction

Rev. Dennis Blackwell,
  Program Co-Chair — New Jersey Annual Conference
Rev. Dr. Dorothy Watson Tatem, — Eastern Pennsylvania Annual
  Evaluation Chair — Conference
Mr. Ernest Swiggett, Finance Chair — New York Annual Conference

South Central Jurisdiction

Rev. Tyrone Gordon, Program Chair — North Texas Annual Conference
Rev. Jackye Waiters-Lee, Secretary — North Texas Annual Conference
Mr. Booker Leeks (2001–2002) — Kansas West Annual Conference
Mr. Ralph Thompson (2003–2004) — South Texas Annual Conference

Southeastern Jurisdiction

Mrs. Rubielee L. Addison — South Carolina Annual Conference
Rev. Helen Davis Bell — Tennessee Annual Conference
Mr. Curtis Henderson — Alabama/West Florida
    Annual Conference

Western Jurisdiction

Mrs. Cheryl Estrada — California-Pacific Annual Conference
Mr. Bobby McCray — Desert Southwest Annual Conference
Rev. James McCray — California-Nevada Annual Conference

BMCR Representative

Rev. McCallister Hollins(2001) — North Georgia Annual Conference
Rev. Vincent Harris (2002–2004) — Texas Annual Conference
Ms. Anne Fleming Williams — Eastern Pennsylvania
    Annual Conference

Appendix B

Youth Representatives

Mr. Henry Stewart — Baltimore-Washington Annual Conference

Ms. Jenna Marie Williams — Nebraska Annual Conference

Young Adult Representatives

Dr. Larry Hygh, Jr. Communication Chair — Baltimore-Washington Annual Conference

Ms. Gabrielle Mallory — West Ohio Annual Conference

SBC21 Staff

Mrs. Cheryl Stevenson, National Coordinator — Kansas West Annual Conference

Ms. Rebecca Brown, Assistant to National Coordinator

Dr. Linda Crowell, Follow Up Consultant — East Ohio Annual Conference

1996-2000 QUARDRENNIUM
COORDINATING COMMITTEE MEMBERS

Episcopal Representation

Bishop Jonathan D. Keaton, Chair	North Central Jurisdiction	East Ohio Area
Bishop Peter D. Weaver	Northeastern Jurisdiction	Philadelphia Area

North Central Jurisdiction   **Annual Conference**

Dr. Carolyn E. Johnson, Vice Chair	North Indiana Annual Conference
Rev. Benita Rollins	East Ohio Annual Conference
Ms. Monique Long	North Illinois Annual Conference

Northeast Jurisdiction

Rev. Dennis Blackwell	New Jersey Annual Conference
Mr. Ernest L. Swiggett, Finance Chair	New York Annual Conference
Ms. Judith C. Hill	Central Pennsylvania Annual Conference

South Central Jurisdiction

Rev. Tyrone D. Gordon	Kansas West Annual Conference
Mrs. Jackye Waiters-Lee	North Texas Annual Conference
Rev. Juanita Rasmus	Texas Annual Conference
Ms. Sara Simmons, Communication Vice Chair (1996)	Omaha, NE
Dr. Charles W. Donaldson (1996)	

Southeastern Jurisdiction

Curtis Henderson, Finance Vice Chair	Alabama/West Florida Annual Conference
Rev. Dr. Walter L. Kimbrough	North Georgia Annual Conference
Mrs. Valerie J. Earvin, Secretary (Dec'd)	North Georgia Annual Conference
Rev. Dr. Walter McKelvey	Gammon Theological Seminary

Western Jurisdiction

Mr. Bobby McCray	Desert Southwest Annual Conference
Rev. James McCray, Jr.	California-Nevada Annual Conference
Ms. Gaunnie Dixon	California-Pacific Annual Conference

Mr. Aaron M. Gray (1996)
Mr. Robert Johnson, Program Vice Chair &
   & Communication Chair (1996)

BMCR Representative
Ms. Anne Fleming Williams   Eastern Pennsylvania Annual
                                   Conference

SBC21 Staff
Ms. Andris Y. Salters, National Coordinator
Ms. Rebecca Brown, Secretary

1992–1996 STUDY PANEL

Bishop Woodie W. White, Chairperson
Dr. Douglas Fitch
Dr. Gilbert Caldwell
Dr. Karen Collier
Rev. Tyrone Gordon
Dr. Carolyn Johnson
Rev. Dolores Queen
Mr. Ernest Swiggett
Dr. Peter Weaver
Dr. Trudie Kibbe Reed, GCOM Administrative Staff

Resource Persons

Rev. Dr. Walter Kimbrough
Ms. Ruth M. Lawson
Rev. Delano McIntosh
Ms. Nelda Barrett Murraine, GCOM
Dr. David White

APPENDIX C: AFRICAN AMERICAN PROGRAM RESOURCES

2005–2008 QUADRENNIUM

RESOURCE PERSON	GENERAL AGENCY
Ms. Newtonia Coleman	United Methodist Communications
Rev. Dr. Fred Allen	United Methodist Publishing House
Ms. Frances Jett	General Board of Church & Society
Ms. Cheryl Walker	General Board of Discipleship
Ms. Diane Johnson	General Board of Global Ministries
Rev. Marion Jackson (2005)	General Board of Higher Education & Ministry
Rev. Clarence Brown	General Board of Higher Education & Ministry
Mr. Ronald Coleman	General Board of Pension & Health Benefits
Rev. James C. Fields, Jr.	General Commission on Christian Unity & Interreligious Concerns
Ms. Erin Hawkins	General Commission on Religion & Race
Ms. Mary White	General Commission on the Status & Role of Women
Rev. Andrea Middleton King	General Commission on United Methodist Men
Mrs. Clauzell Williams	General Council on Finance & Administration
Rev. Carl Arrington	Southeastern Jurisdiction Administration Council

NEWS COVERAGE
Ms. Linda Green, United Methodist News Service

2001–2004 QUADRENNIUM

RESOURCE PERSON	GENERAL AGENCY
Ms. Newtonia Coleman	United Methodist Communications
Rev. Dr. Fred Allen	United Methodist Publishing House
Mr. Cedric Foley	United Methodist Publishing House
Ms. Frances Jett	General Board of Church & Society
Ms. Annette Vanzant Williams (2003)	General Board of Church & Society
Ms. Marilyn Magee (2001–2003)	General Board of Discipleship
Rev. Francine Taylor-Thirus (2004)	General Board of Discipleship
Ms. Ruth Lawson (2001–2003)	General Board of Global Ministries
Ms. Diane Johnson (2004)	General Board of Global Ministries
Rev. Lillian Smith	General Board of Higher Education & Ministry
Ms. Barbara Boigegrain (2001)	General Board of Pensions & Health Benefits
Ms. Kimberly Vantrease(2001–2002)	General Board of Pension & Health Benefits
Mr. Ronald Coleman (2003–2004)	General Board of Pension & Health Benefits
Dr. Charles Yrigoyen, Jr.	General Commission on Archives & History
Rev. James C. Fields, Jr.	General Commission on Christian Unity & Interreligious Concerns
Rev. Chester R. Jones (2001)	General Commission on Religion & Race
Ms. Erin Hawkins (2002–2004)	General Commission on Religion & Race
Ms. Mary White (2002)	General Commission on the Status & Role of Women
Rev. Andrea Middleton King	General Commission on United Methodist Men
Rev. Robert Smith (2001–2003)	General Council on Finance & Administration
Mrs. Clauzell Williams (2004)	General Council on Finance & Administration
Mrs. Nelda Barrett Murraine (2001–2003)	General Council on Ministries
Ms. Cecelia Long (2003–2004)	General Council on Ministries
Ms. Cheryl Walker	Southeastern Jurisdiction Administration Council

NEWS COVERAGE
Ms. Linda Green, United Methodist News Service

1996–2000 QUADRENNIUM

RESOURCE PERSON	GENERAL AGENCY
Newtonia Coleman	United Methodist Communications
Cynthia Gadsden	United Methodist Publishing House
Shanta M. Bryant	General Board of Church & Society
Marilyn W. Magee	General Board of Discipleship
Dr. Roderick McLean	General Board of Global Ministries
Thomas Robinson	General Board of Global Ministries
Delano M. McIntosh	General Board of Higher Education & Ministry
Rev. Lillian Smith	General Board of Higher Education & Ministry
Dr. Charles Yrigoyen, Jr.	General Commission on Archived & History
Dr. Rhymes H. Moncure, Jr. (Dec'd)	General Commission on Christian Unity and Interreligious Concerns
Constance Nelson-Barnes	General Commission on Religion & Race
Elaine Jenkins	General Commission on Religion & Race
Cecelia Long	General Commission on the Status & Role of Women
Kevin James	General Commission on United Methodist Men
Rev. Robert Smith	General Council on Finance & Administration
C. David Lundquist	General Council on Ministries (General Secretary)
Nelda Barrett Murraine	General Council on Ministries
Linda Bales	General Council on Ministries (Staff Consultant)
Cheryl Walker	Southeastern Jurisdiction Administration Council
Dale Patterson (1997)	

NEWS COVERAGE
Linda Green, United Methodist News Service

APPENDIX D: CRC LISTING

2005-2008 QUADRENNIUM
CONGREGATION RESOURCE CENTERS

JURISDICTION

	Pastor	Location	Conference	Category
North Central				
Aldersgate UMC	Rev. Julius C. Trimble	Warrensville, OH	East Ohio	Suburban
St. Mark UMC	Rev. Jon McCoy	Chicago, IL	North Central	Urban
Northeastern				
Asbury UMC	Rev. Dennis Blackwell	Merchantville, NJ	Southern New Jersey	Suburban
Brooks Memorial UMC	Rev. John T. Simmons (Rev. John Carrington, retired 2006)	Jamaica, NY	New York	Urban
Eastwick Worship Center	Rev. Harry Benson	Philadelphia, PA	Eastern Pennsylvania	Urban
Emory UMC	Rev. Joseph Daniels, Jr.	Washington, DC	Baltimore-Washington	Urban
South Central				
St. John's UMC	Rev. Rudy & Juanita Rasmus	Houston, TX	Texas	Urban
St. Luke Community UMC	Rev. Tyrone D. Gordon	Dallas, TX	North Texas	Urban
Saint Mark UMC	Rev. Junius Dotson	Wichita, KS	Kansas West	Urban

Church	Pastor	City	Conference	Type
Theressa Hoover UMC	Rev. William Robinson, Jr.	Little Rock, AR	Arkansas	Urban
Windsor Village UMC	Rev. Kirbyjon Caldwell	Houston, TX	Texas	Urban
Southeastern				
Bennettsville Cheraw Area Cooperative Ministry	Rev. Stephen Love	Bennettsville, SC	South Carolina	Rural
Cascade UMC	Rev. Walter Kimbrough (retired 2006)	Atlanta, GA	North Georgia	Urban
New Life Community	Rev. Candace M. Lewis	Jacksonville, FL	Florida	Suburban
St. Thomas Charge UMC (New Hope, Steward Chapel, Zion)	Rev. Marvin Taylor	Huger, SC	South Carolina	Rural
Wesley UMC	Rev. Edgar Goins	Lexington, KY	Kentucky	Urban
South Columbus UMC	Rev. Joseph Roberson	Columbus, SC	South Georgia	Urban
Western				
Glide UMC	Rev. Douglas Fitch	San Francisco, CA	California-Nevada	Urban
Holman UMC	Rev. Henry Masters, Sr.	Los Angeles, CA	California-Pacific	Urban
Zion UMC	Rev. Percell Church, Jr.	Las Vegas, NV	Desert	Urban

2001–2004 QUADRENNIUM

CONGREGATION RESOURCE CENTERS

JURISDICTION	Pastor	Location	Conference	Category
North Central				
Aldersgate UMC	Rev. Benita Rollins	Warrensville, OH	East Ohio	Suburban
Hope UMC	Rev. Carlyle F. Stewart, III	Southfield, MI	Detroit	Suburban
Northeastern				
AP Shaw UMC	Rev. Ernest D. Lyles, Sr.	Washington, DC	Baltimore-Washington	Urban
Asbury UMC	Rev. Dennis L. Blackwell	Merchantville, NJ	Southern NJ	Suburban
Brooks Memorial UMC	Rev. John E. Carrington	Jamaica, NY	New York	Urban
Eastwick UMC	Rev. Helen Stafford Fleming	Philadelphia, PA	Eastern Pennsyvania	Urban
Emory UMC	Rev. Joseph Daniels, Jr.	Washington, DC	Baltimore-Washington	Urban
John Wesley UMC	Rev. Alfreda Wiggins	Baltimore, MD	Baltimore-Washington	Urban
South Central				
St. John's UMC	Rev. Rudy & Juanita Rasmus	Houston, TX	Texas	Urban
St. Luke Community UMC	Rev. Tyrone D. Gordon	Dallas, TX	North Texas	Urban

Saint Mark UMC	Rev. Junius Dotson	Wichita, KS	Kansas West	Urban
Theressa Hoover UMC	Rev. William H. Robinson, Jr.	Little Rock, AR	Arkansas	Urban
Windsor Village UMC	Rev. Kirbyjon Caldwell	Houston, TX	Texas	Urban

Southeastern

Ben Hill UMC	Rev. McCallister Hollins	Atlanta, GA	North Georgia	Urban
Bennettsville Cheraw Area Cooperative Ministry	Rev. Edward McKnight	Bennettsville, SC	South Carolina	Rural
Francis Burns UMC	Rev. Mack McClam	Columbia, SC	South Carolina	Suburban
New Life Community	Rev. Candace M. Lewis	Jacksonville, FL	Florida	Suburban
North Orangeburg UMC	Rev. Eddie C. Williams	Orangeburg, SC	South Carolina	Suburban
Ousley UMC	Rev. Michael McQueen	Lithonia, GA	North Georgia	Suburban
St. Thomas Charge UMC (New Hope, Steward Chapel, Zion)	Rev. Marvin Taylor	Huger, SC	South Carolina	Rural

Western

Crossroads/ Njia Panda	Rev. Lydia J. Waters	Compton, CA	California-Pacific	Urban
Downs Memorial UMC	Rev. Kelvin Sauls	Oakland, CA	California-Nevada	Urban

1996-2000 QUADRENNIUM

CONGREGATION RESOURCE CENTERS

JURISDICTION

	Pastor	Location	Conference	Category
North Central				
Aldersgate UMC	Rev. Neriah Edwards	Warrensville, OH	East Ohio	Suburban
Barnes UMC	Rev. Charles R. Harrison	Indianapolis, IN	South Indiana	Urban
Hope UMC	Rev. Carlyle F. Stewart, III	Southfield, MI	Detroit	Suburban
Maple Park/ Gorham UM	Rev. Larry D. Pickens	Chicago, IL	North Illinois	Urban
Wesley UMC	Rev. Larry Martin	Jeffersonville, IN	South Indiana	Urban
Northeastern				
A.P. Shaw UMC	Rev. Kenneth Greene (Dec'd)	Washington, DC	Baltimore-Washington	Urban
Congress Heights UMC	Rev. Sandra Greene	Washington	Baltimore-Washington	
Asbury UMC	Rev. Dennis Blackwell	Merchantville, NJ	Southern New Jersey	Suburban

Church	Pastor	City	Conference	Type
Brooks Memorial UMC	Rev. Joseph Washington	Jamaica, NY	New York	Urban
John Wesley UMC	Rev. Alfreda Wiggins	Baltimore, MD	Baltimore-Washington	Urban
Resurrection Prayer Worship Center UMC	Rev. Anthony Muse	Brandywine, MD	Baltimore-Washington	Rural
South Central				
St. James Paseo UMC	Rev. Emanuel Cleaver, II	Kansas City, KS	Missouri West	Urban
St. John UMC	Rev. Rudy & Juanita Rasmus	Houston, TX	Texas	Urban
Saint Mark UMC	Rev. Tyrone D. Gordon	Wichita, KS	Kansas West	Urban
Theressa Hoover UMC	Rev. William H. Robinson, Jr.	Little Rock, AR	Little Rock	Urban
Windsor Village UMC	Rev. Kirbyjon Caldwell	Houston, TX	Texas	Urban
Southeastern				
Ben Hill UMC	Rev. McAllister Hollins	Atlanta, GA	North Georgia	Urban
Bennettsville-Cheraw Area Cooperative Ministry	Rev. Samuel Cooper Rev. Alfred Griffin	Bennettsville, SC	South Carolina	Rural
Cascade UMC	Rev. Walter Kimbrough	Atlanta, GA	North Georgia	Urban
Francis Burns UMC	Rev. Mack McClam	Columbia, SC	South Carolina	Suburban

H.A. Brown Memorial	Rev. Carolyn Abrams	Wiggins, MS	Mississippi	Rural
Mt. Pleasant UMC	Rev. Geraldine McClellan	Gainesville, FL	Florida	Urban
North Orangeburg UMC	Rev. Calvin Alston, Jr.	Orangeburg, SC	South Carolina	Suburban

Western

Crossroads/ Njia Panda	Rev. Lydia Jackson Waters	Compton, CA	California-Pacific	Urban
Downs Memorial UMC	Rev. Douglas Fitch	Oakland, CA	California-Nevada	Urban
Genesis UMC	Rev. Junius Dotson	Milpitas, CA	California-Pacific	Suburban

APPENDIX E

Congregational-Community
Profile Form

Please answer the following questions.

Date: _____

Pastor's Name: _____

Church Name: _____

Address: _____

City: _____State: ___ Zip Code: _____ P.O.B. _____

Jurisdiction:_____Conference:_____District_____

Telephone Number: _____ Fax: _____

E-mail Address: _____

Membership Size: _____

☐ Rural   ☐ Suburban   ☐ Urban

Partner Church Team: Please list the 5-member Partner Church Team (Pastor & Lay) that will attend SBC21 Training. The pastor must attend training with the PC Team.

Name   **Ministry**

1)_____ (pastor)   _____

2)_____   _____

3)_____   _____

4)_____   _____

5)_____   _____

Pastor's Signature: _____ _____ Date: _____

Please return to:

Strengthening the Black Church for the 21st Century
General Board of Discipleship
P.O. Box 340003
Nashville, TN 37203-0003
Toll Free #: 877-899-2780, ext. 1722
Email: cstevenson@gbod.org FAX: 615-340-7071

(Please complete the Congregational-Community Profile Questions on the reverse side of this form.)

CONGREGATIONAL-COMMUNITY PROFILE QUESTIONS

Share with us your church history? How does your history and heritage impact your ministry?

What is the mission of your church? Do you have a mission and/or vision statement? What are they?

Please list and explain any ministries/programs within your church.

Identify the strengths, weaknesses, opportunities, and challenges of the congregation's ministry?

Who lives in the community surrounding your church? What is the church involvement in the community? How is the community reflected within your congregation?

How does your congregation understand its role in the community?

What are the demographics of your congregation? What are the demographics of your community relative to the Pre-Christian (unchurched)?

What critical needs have you identified within your community that are not addressed by others?

Appendix F
United Methodist Church Websites

WWW.SBC21.org	(Strengthening The Black for the 21st Century)
WWW.bmcrumc.org	(Black Methodists for Church Renewal)
WWW.gcfa.org	(General Council on Finance and Administration)
WWW.umc-gbcs.org	(General Board of Church and Society)
WWW.gbod.org	(General Board of Discipleship)
WWW.gbgm-umc.org	(General Board of Global Ministries)
WWW.gbhem.org	(General Board of Higher Education and Ministry)
WWW.gbophb.org	(General Board of Pension and Health Benefits)
WWW.umph.org	(The United Methodist Publishing House)
WWW.gcah.org	(General Commission on Archives and History)
WWW.gccuic-umc.org	(General Commission on Christian Unity and Interreligious Concerns)
WWW.umcom.org	(United Methodist Communications)
WWW.gcorr.org	(General Commission on Religion and Race)
WWW.gcsrw.org	(General Commission on the Status and Role of Women
WWW.gcumm.org	(General Commission on United Methodist Men)
WWW.umc.org	(The United Methodist Church)
WWW.cokesbury.org	(Cokesbury Internet Bookstore)

APPENDIX G

Directory of United Methodist "Ebony" Bishops
(Active & Retired)

Edsel A. Ammons*
Warner H. Brown, Jr.
Violet L. Fisher
Alfred Johnson*
Charles Wesley Jordon*
Jonathan D. Keaton
Leontine T. C. Kelly*
James R. King, Jr.
Linda Lee
Ernest S. Lyght
Marcus Matthews

Felton Edwin May*
William W. Morris*
Alfred Norris*
Gregory Vaughn Palmer
Beverly J. Shamana
Herbert F. Skeete*
Forrest C. Stith*
James E. Swanson, Sr.
Melvin G. Talbert*
James S. Thomas*
Woodie W. White*

Bishops in the Central Conference of Africa

Benjamin Boni (Côte d'Ivoire)
Gaspar Joao Domingos (West Angola, DRC)
Moises Domingos Fernandes (Angola)*
Joseph C. Humper (Sierra Leone)
John G. Innis (Liberia)
Kainda Katembo (South Congo, DRC)
Joao Somane Machado (Mozambique)
Kefas Kane Mavula (Nigeria)
Abel T. Muzorewa (Zimbabwe)*
Eben Nhiwatiwa (Zimbabwe)
Nkulu Ntanda Ntambo (North Katanga, DRC)
Fama Onema (DRC)*
Jose Quipungo (East Angola)
Daniel Wandabula (East Africa Area)
David K. Yemba (Central Congo, DRC)

(Retired*)

BIBLIOGRAPHY

Asmal, Kader, Chedesta, David, and James, Wilmot eds. *Nelson Mandela: In His Own Words*. London: Little Brown, 2003.

Barnes, Thelma P. "Through the Years," in *Our Time Under God Is Now*. Woodie White, ed. Nashville: Abingdon Press, 1993.

Baketel, Oliver S., ed. *The Methodist Yearbook, 1913*. Nashville: The Methodist Publishing House, 1913.

_____, ed. 1914. *The Methodist Yearbook, 1914*. The Methodist Publishing House.

_____, ed. 1916. *The Methodist Yearbook, 1916*. The Methodist Publishing House.

_____, ed. 1930. *The Methodist Yearbook, 1930*. The Methodist Publishing House.

Bordewich, Fergus M. *Bound for Canaan: The Underground Railroad and the War for the Soul of America*. New York: HarperCollins, 2005.

Briddell, David. Report on Strengthening the Black Church for the 21st Century, 2004 General Conference, 2005–2008.

Caldwell, Kirbyjon H. *The Gospel of Good Success: A Road Map to Spiritual, Emotional and Financial Wholeness*. New York: Simon and Schuster, 1999.

Calkin, Homer L. *Castings from the Foundry Mold: A History of Foundry Church Washington, D.C. 1814–1964*. Nashville: Parthenon Press, 1968.

The Committee of Five. Study Document on Realignment of the Central Jurisdiction to the 1964 General Conference. 1964.

Cole, Johnnetta B. Last Word: "Six Steps to Effective Leadership," *Black Issues in Higher Education*. October 24, 2002.

Cone, James. *Speaking the Truth: Ecumenism, Liberation, and Black Theology*. Maryknoll, NY: Orbis Books, 1986.

Culver, Dwight. *Negro Segregation in the Methodist Church*. New Haven: Yale University Press, 1953.

Daily Christian Advocate: Advance ed., 1, (1996) General Conference.

Dole, Kenneth. "Minister Cites Unusual Image," *Washington Churchmen*, Washington Post, August 10, 1968.

Dubois, W.E.B. *The Soul of Black Folks*. New York: Bantam Books, 1989.

Dumbarton United Methodist Church. Mount Zion Is Born. *Dumbarton United Methodist Church Cookbook: Seasonings of the Spirit*. http://wwww.dumbarton-umc.org/cookbook.

Easum, William M. and Bandy, Thomas G. *Growing Spiritual Redwoods*. Nashville: Abingdon Press, 1997.

"Eight Decades of Brooks Memorial History and Memories." Unpublished, Brooks Memorial United Methodist Church. Jamaica, New York, 2004.

Fisher, Margaret. "A History of Emory Methodist Church 1832–1962: One Hundred and Thirtieth Anniversary." Unpublished, 1962.

Franklin, John Hope. *From Slavery to Freedom: A History of Negro Americans*, 5th ed. New York: Alfred A. Knopf, 1980.

Franklin, Robert M. *Another Day's Journey*. Minneapolis, MN: Fortress Press, 1997.

_____. *Crisis in the Village*. Minneapolis: Fortress Press, 2007.

_____. *Liberating Visions: Human Fulfillment and Social Justice in African-American Thought*. Minneapolis, MN: Fortress Press, 1990.

General Board of Discipleship, "Fifty Characteristics of Disciple-Making Congregations." Dean McIntyre, www.GBOD.org, 2004; http:// www.umcworship.org.

General Commission on Archives and History. "Zoar United Methodist Church, Philadelphia, Pennsylvania: Heritage Landmark of The Untied Methodist Church." http://www.gcah.org/Heritage_Landmarks/Zoar.htm.

General Commission on Religion and Race. Black Concerns. http://www.gcorr.org/committee_files?BlackConstituency/concerns.htm.

Harding, Vincent. *There Is a River: The Black Struggle for Freedom in America*. New York: Harcourt Brace Jovanovich, 1991.

Keaton, Jonathan D., chairperson. "Strengthening The Black Church for the 21st Century Spring 2006 Progress Report." Unpublished, 2006.

Kirk, W. Astor. *Desegregation of the Methodist Church Polity: Reform Movements that Ended Racial Segregation*. Pittsburgh: RoseDog Books, 2005.

Kline, Marvin. "History of Rohrersville United Methodist Church." Unpublished, 1971.

Knight, Hal III. *Eight Life-Enriching Practices of United Methodists*. Nashville: Abingdon Press, 2001.

Knight, Hal III and Powe, F. Douglas. *Transforming Evangelism: The Wesleyan Way of Sharing Faith*. Nashville: Discipleship Resources, 2006.

Lawson, James M. "The Early Days," in *Our Time Under God Is Now*. Woodie White, ed. Nashville: Abingdon Press, 1993.

Lewis, Robert and Cordeiro, Wayne, with Bird, Warren. *Culture Shift: Transforming Your Church from the Inside Out*. San Francisco, CA: JosseyBass, 2005.

The Lexington Conference, Central Jurisdiction. Philadelphia: Division of National Mission, 1957.

Lincoln, Eric C. and Mamiya, Lawrence H. *The Black Church in the African American Experience*. Durham: Duke University Press, 1990.

Matthaei, Sondra. *Making Disciples: Faith Formation in the Wesleyan Tradition*. Nashville: Abingdon Press, 2000.

McClain, William B. *Black People in the Methodist Church*. Nashville: Abingdon, 1984.

_____. "The Story of Songs of Zion: Pioneering Paths in a Strange Land." Unpublished paper, 2005.

McMickle, Marvin A. *Preaching to the Black Middle Class: Words of Challenge, Words of Hope.* Valley Forge, PA: Judson Press, 2000.

Mitchem, Stephanie Y. *Introducing Womanist Theology.* Marynoll, NY: Orbis Books, 2002.

Nichols, Roy C. *Doing the Gospel: Local Congregations in Ministry.* Nashville: Abingdon Press, 1990.

Norwood, Frederick A. *The Story of American Methodism: A History of the United Methodists and Their Relations.* Nashville: Abingdon Press, 1974.

Pembroke, June. "The St. Mark Story: A Brief Sketch of the St. Mark UMC Heritage." Unpublished, 2004.

Rasmus, Rudy. *Touch: The Power of Touch in Transforming Lives.* Houston: Baxter Press and Spirit Rising Music, 2006.

Reiland, Dan. *Shoulder to Shoulder: Strengthening Your Church by Supporting Your Pastor.* Nashville: Thomas Nelson Inc., 1997.

Report on Strengthening the Black Church for the 21st Century," Report No. 3. Petition Number: 21677-GJ-NonDis-OS; GCOM, 1996, 1996 General Conference, 1997–2000.

Richey, Russell E. *Early American Methodism.* Bloomington and Indianapolis: Indiana University Press, 1991.

"Rites of Passage: Ministry, Music, and Mosaics: The 165th Anniversary of Emory United Methodist Church Washington, DC, Commemorative Edition 1997," Unpublished.

Saint Paul United Methodist Church. "The History of St. Paul United Methodist Church," http://www.stpumcmd.org/history3.htm.

St. John's Downtown. "Blueprint Church: St. John's United Methodist Church." Christian Washington, August 25, 2002, www.stjohnsdowntown.org.

Stewart, Carlyle Fielding III. *African American Church Growth: 12 Principles of Prophetic Ministry.* Nashville: Abingdon Press, 1994.

_____. *The Empowerment Church.* Nashville: Abingdon Press, 2001.

Stith, Forest and Wallace, Horace, compliers. "African American Methodist Church History: Key Dates." Unpublished, 2006.

Straker, Ian B. "Black and White and Gray All Over: Freeborn Garrettson and American Methodism." *Methodist History* (1998) 37.1:18–17.

Stukenbroeker, Fern C. *A Watermelon for God: A History of Trinity United Methodist Church, Alexandria, Virginia, 1774–1974.* Alexandria, VA, 1974.

Swanson, Roger K. and Clement, Shirley F. *Faith-Sharing Congregation.* Nashville: Abingdon Books, 2002.

Talbert, Marilyn Magee. *The Past Matters: A Chronology of African Americans in The United Methodist Church.* Nashville: Discipleship Resources, 2005.

Temple United Methodist Church. "African American Pioneers in the United Methodist Church," by Barbara Brown, February 4, 2001. http://www.templeumc.org/archives/Black_Pioneers.html.

Thomas, James S. *Methodism's Racial Dilemma: The Story of the Central Jurisdiction.* Nashville: Abingdon Press, 1992.

Thompson, Barbara Ricks. "The United Methodist Church's View of the Significance of BMCR," in *Our Time Under God Is Now.* Woodie White, ed. Nashville: Abingdon Press, 1993.

United Methodist Church. "African Americans Gather to Remember Central Jurisdiction," by Pamela Crosby, 2004.

_____. "Center Will Document History of African-American Methodists."

_____. "Commentary: Reunion Provides Time to Reflect on Segregated Era, by Rev. Gilbert H. Caldwell.

United Methodist News Service. "Songs of Zion Opened Doors for Songs of Soul and Soil." June 13, 2005, http://archives.umc.org/interior.asp?ptid=2&mid=8953.

Warren, Rick. *The Purpose Driven Church: Growth Without Compromising Your Message and Mission.* Grand Rapids, Mich.: Zondervan, 1995.

Weber, Theodore. *Politics in the Order of Salvation.* Nashville: Kingswood Books, 2001.

Wesley, John. "On Visiting the Sick," *Works 3.* Nashville: Abingdon Press, 1986.